MISSION ACCOMPLISHED!

MARLON R. HALL
4658 E. ILLINOIS
FRESNO, CA 93702
209-252-8464

Printing by: Eerdmans Printing Company, Grand Rapids, Michigan

MISSION ACCOMPLISHED!
Michigan's Basketball Miracle, 1989

by
JOHN BECKETT

with photographs by
DUANE BLACK
and
a foreword by
BO SCHEMBECHLER

DIAMOND COMMUNICATIONS, INC.

SOUTH BEND, INDIANA

1989

MISSION ACCOMPLISHED!
Copyright © 1989 by Diamond Communications, Inc.

Manufactured in the United States of America

DIAMOND COMMUNICATIONS, INC.
POST OFFICE BOX 88
SOUTH BEND, INDIANA 46624
(219) 287–5008

Library of Congress Cataloging-in-Publication Data

Beckett, John, 1950 May 19–
   Mission accomplished! : Michigan's basketball miracle, 1989 / by
John Beckett : with photographs by Duane Black.
      p.   cm.
   ISBN 0–912083–42–5 : $25.00 — ISBN 0–912083–41–7 (pbk.) : $12.95
   1. University of Michigan—Basketball.   2. National Collegiate
Athletic Association Basketball Tournament.   I. Title.
GV885.43.U536B43   1989   89–36690
796.323'63'0977435—dc20   CIP

Contents

For my father and mother,
who taught me to appreciate the beauty
of both sports and the written word.

Foreword

We have a saying at Michigan. It's on a plaque over the doorway to my office, and it says, "Those who stay will be champions." This is a statement that demonstrates a commitment to excellence, a commitment we seek from all of our athletes. In return, we offer them the same commitment. If they come to Michigan and dedicate themselves to excellence, we will do the same, with the hope and belief that most of them will experience, during their Michigan careers, the honor of being champions of some sort.

Perhaps no Michigan team ever lived up to that saying better than the national championship basketball team of 1989. Faced with the loss of their coach on the eve of the NCAA Tournament, they pulled together, concentrated, executed, and at the bottom line played some brilliant basketball to give Michigan its first national basketball championship. Coach Steve Fisher and his Wolverines earned themselves a spot in the history books with their performance. I've been around a long time, and this championship will go down as one of the great accomplishments in Michigan athletic history, and as one of the most memorable stories in the 51-year history of the NCAA Tournament.

John Beckett has a fine vantage point from which to tell that story. As Michigan basketball reporter for the *Ann Arbor News* for the last four seasons, he has probably been closer to the program than any other reporter.

The team he covered was a pretty darn good one, even before last April. I don't claim to be an authority on basketball, but I know the game a little. And I know athletes. And Steve Fisher had some athletes. I would have been one happy football coach if Rumeal Robinson had ever walked into my office and told me he had decided to play defensive back. He could be a great cornerback. Then you've got a big guy like Terry Mills. When teams start pushing, this big boy can hold his own. You put 25 or 30 pounds on him and I'll have him playing tackle for me. And they had Loy Vaught and Mark Hughes, pretty good bruisers in their own right. And there's Mike Griffin. This kid can really take a punch. He's the best I've seen at taking one on the jaw. And for scorers? Sean Higgins, who is my favorite player, and Glen Rice—who scored more points than any other player in Big Ten and NCAA Tournament history. Plus the supporting players, from the off-the-bench contributors like Demetrius Calip to the unsung heroes like Kirk Taylor and J.P. Oosterbaan.

So, Steve Fisher had a lot to work with. But he took over under a helluva tough set of circumstances. I thought he did a wonderful job; I was tremendously proud of his performance in the tournament.

Some people criticized me for taking a little time in giving Steve the head coach's job. But I don't make decisions very quickly, and I wasn't about to make this one during the great emotion of that tournament. But I know I made the right choice. Steve Fisher shares the same feeling that I do, that you play the game for the guys who play; that the players are the ones who count the most. I think Steve is a good teacher, a man who works well with young people. In the tournament, it was a different Michigan team. They played with enthusiasm, they knew where they were going, and they knew what they had to do. I've seen other Michigan teams not respond to tough situations like this one did. Somebody had to be responsible for that, and I figure it was Steve Fisher. Of course, he's going to lose sometime. The honeymoon won't last forever. So far, everything that's been said or written has been in adulation of Steve Fisher. And I know full well it doesn't work out that way. You don't win a national championship every year. It takes a tough guy to be a coach. You have to be very thick-skinned. But I think that, underneath that nice-guy exterior, Steve Fisher can be one tough guy. And I believe he will give us a new, fresh, exciting era of Michigan basketball.

Of course, it will be difficult to come up with anything more exciting than last season's finish. It was one of the great achievements of our storied athletic history, and the good feelings and wonderful memories it provided to players, coaches, and fans are beyond value. It was what college athletics are supposed to be all about. Like that saying on our wall, the 1989 Michigan Wolverines gave us, all of us, something to shoot for.

Bo Schembechler
Ann Arbor, Michigan
July 1989

Author's Note

They say that to win a championship, it's just as important to be lucky as it is to be good. That also holds true for writing about championships. Nearly five years ago, I was fortunate enough to be assigned to cover the Michigan Wolverines, who were expected to challenge for the national championship that season. Unfortunately, former Michigan man Johnny Orr and his Iowa State Cyclones had other ideas, and the Wolverines were upset in the second round of the NCAA Tournament. However, that was the same season that Glen Rice, Mark Hughes, Loy Vaught, Mike Griffin, and J.P. Oosterbaan arrived on the scene, and just one year before Terry Mills and Rumeal Robinson came to Michigan. It would take four years but the timing was perfect to watch the development of a national championship team.

The timing was also right to watch the demise of coach Bill Frieder, whose Michigan popularity was peaking at about the time I began covering the team. Years from now, people will look back at Frieder's record and wonder how fans could possibly have been displeased with him. In some ways, it remains something of a mystery to me, even after watching it, as Steve Fisher would say, "up close and personal." It was an ironic story. Perhaps the greatest irony was that Frieder, who hated being described as a great recruiter but only an average bench coach, seemed to prove with his departure just how true the label was. I have tried to describe, and perhaps partially explain, the dynamics of the situation. But I think it will remain something of a "You had to be there" story.

That I was there is something for which I'll always be thankful. That I was there for every game of Glen Rice's marvelous career, that I got to know fascinating characters like Bill Frieder, Rumeal Robinson, and Sean Higgins. I'll always consider myself lucky, not only to have covered a national championship team, but to have gotten to know people like Terry Mills, Mark

Hughes, Loy Vaught, and all the rest of the Wolverines, their coaches, and their families.

This is a story about the Wolverines. It's a story about college basketball, so it's a story about statistics, about scores, about points, rebounds, turnovers, and wins and losses. But college basketball is much more than that. It's people: young men dreaming of professional careers; young men financing their educations by playing a game they love; and middle-aged men whose high-paying, high-profile jobs depend on getting 18-to-21-year-olds to play that game well. College basketball is also a dream: the dream of making it to the Final Four, the dream of winning it all. It's a dream that touches the lives of thousands of players, coaches, officials, and millions of fans. But more than anything, college basketball is a game. *The* game, perhaps, of the 1980s and 1990s. It has become an enormously popular entertainment, an enormously lucrative business. But it remains, at bottom line, a game. It is a beautiful game partly because of its unique blending of the individual player and the team. It allows players great individual freedom and rewards individual skills, but what it really values are players who learn how and when to sacrifice some of their freedom and individuality for the good of the team. That is one of the greatest lessons of college basketball, and one of the hardest to learn. It was a lesson the Michigan Wolverines needed to learn to win the national championship, and one they did learn. That they finally did was no surprise to those of us who covered the team regularly. The Wolverines' talent was always obvious, just as the suggestion that they were lazy or selfish was always wrong. Michigan won the national title in 1989 because the Wolverines were a talented, aggressive, intelligent, unselfish team—qualities instilled by Frieder, Fisher, and their staff, who never really received the credit they deserved, even after Michigan won it all.

Although some readers may disagree, I think this is a story without any villains. It is a story of people—players, coaches, and administrators—caught up in the sometimes surprising, sometimes saddening, sometimes joyous stew that simmers in the pressure cooker of college basketball. It is the story of a team, and of how its individual players and coaches rose to the greatest challenge of their lives.

Although I was there, in terms of covering the Wolverines for the past four seasons, there obviously were times—such as in huddles, film sessions, at players' homes, etc.—when I wasn't there. Many of the scenes in this book were happenings at which neither I nor any reporter was present. They are in reality reconstructions of scenes, reconstructions gleaned from talking to players, coaches, managers, and others close to the team. These scenes, including quotations, have been drawn from a number of sources, and I have tried to reconstruct them as accurately as possible.

This book would not have been possible without the gracious cooperation that the Michigan Wolverines have shown me for the past four seasons. I extend my thanks to them all, and specifically to coaches Bill Frieder, Steve Fisher, Mike Boyd, Brian Dutcher, Joe Czupek and Jay Smith; Glen Rice, Rumeal Robinson, Loy Vaught, Demetrius Calip, Terry Mills, and Mark Hughes; equipment manager Bob Bland; manager Joel Portnoy; trainer Dan Minert; and Bruce Madej, Mike Murray, and the rest of Michigan's sports information staff. I'd also like to thank Bo Schembechler, Janice Frieder, Jerry Ashby, Professor Howard Brabson, Army coach Les Wothke, Bob Pille of the *Chicago Sun-Times*, and my mentor, Jeff Mortimer. Special thanks go to my publishers, Jill and Jim Langford, and to photographer Duane Black. And the most special thanks of all go to Jean, my wife, and Jessica and Joshua, my children, for putting up with the demented lifestyle of a sportswriter.

John Beckett
Brighton, Michigan
July 1989

About the Author

After having worked as a disc jockey, news reporter, and sportscaster for two years, John Beckett began his career as a newspaper reporter in 1971 and, in 1979, he joined the sports staff of the *Ann Arbor News.* For the last four years Beckett's sportswriting specialty has been Michigan Wolverines basketball. As the U-M beat reporter and columnist, he has covered every Wolverine basketball game through four seasons for the *Ann Arbor News* as well as for seven other Booth newspapers throughout Michigan.

In 1987, the Associated Press Sports Editors presented Beckett with a national first place award in recognition of his series of features on Proposition 48. In addition to this honor, he has received numerous state awards from Associated Press and United Press International. Beckett is an annual contributor to *Big Ten Basketball* magazine and for the fourth straight year serves as one of the voters for the Associated Press' Top 20 College Basketball Poll. His assignments also include coverage of Michigan gridiron play for the *Ann Arbor News,* whose sports section, both daily and Sunday, has enjoyed Top 10 national ranking for the last three years as determined by the Associated Press Sports Editors.

Beckett resides in Brighton, Michigan, with his wife Jean, daughter Jessica, and son Joshua.

The Mission

Indiana guard Lyndon Jones raced upcourt with the ball. Nine seconds remained in the game. Eight, seven, six, five . . . Jones saw backcourt mate Jay Edwards out of the corner of his eye and passed him the ball, between the two circles. Four, three . . . Edwards dribbled, stopped, and squared up to the basket. Two, one . . . as Michigan's 6–9 Sean Higgins lunged desperately at the 6–4 Edwards, he just as desperately fired up a prayerful 24-foot jumper.

Swish!

Indiana 76, Michigan 75.

Edwards, falling backwards on the fadeaway 3-pointer, landed on the seat of his pants on the Assembly Hall floor. Higgins, who had stopped in his tracks to follow the flight of the ball, was for one tiny second the only motionless person in a sea of Hoosier players, cheerleaders, and fans that engulfed their prone hero. Coach Bob Knight, whose team had just all but clinched the 1989 Big Ten championship, bounded around the floor like a little boy, jubilantly throwing both arms into the air.

Michigan players and coaches protested furiously. Surely the basket hadn't counted. Surely the shot had come after time ran out. Coach Bill Frieder stood there with his towel on his shoulder, stunned. Assistant coach Steve Fisher stormed toward the officials, arguing with them.

The score stood: Indiana 76, Michigan 75.

And the more important score stood: Indiana 11–1, Michigan 7–5.

Indiana's sweet victory was Michigan's bitter defeat. With it, the Wolverines realistically lost their last hope of competing for the 1989 Big Ten championship. A team that had been ranked ahead of Indiana for much of the season, a team that had been ranked as high as second, a team picked to contend for the Big Ten title, was out of the running with six games—a full third of the season—remaining.

1

Indiana coach Bob Knight thought Michigan had an excellent team, and he was no fan of the Wolverines.

Michigan coach Bill Frieder, with his ever-present towel.

In the lockerroom, the Wolverines were furious. How had they let this game—and this season—slip away from them?

They had overcome so many obstacles, battled back so many times. All afternoon, throughout the nationally-televised game in Indiana's fearsome Assembly Hall, the Wolverines had scratched and clawed to stay with the Hoosiers.

Indiana, which usually used screens to free up its jump-shooters, had switched tactics from the outset, driving around screens instead of shooting from behind them. All three guards were looking to drive at every opportunity, especially whenever they found themselves guarded by Glen Rice or Rumeal Robinson. The changeup caught the Wolverines off-guard defensively, and meant early foul trouble for three key players—Rice, Robinson, and Mike Griffin, who eventually fouled out.

It seemed Michigan had to battle not only the Indiana team, but the officials, too. In the first half, five of the first six fouls were called on Michigan. Rice, the Big Ten's leading scorer, headed for the bench with his third foul with 3:18 left to play. One minute into the second half, Rice was whistled for his fourth foul. Seven of the first eight whistles that half also went against Michigan. Yet after Loy Vaught and Terry Mills hit back-to-back baskets with nine minutes remaining, Michigan had a 60–57 lead.

Rice had been—and would be, when he returned with eight minutes left—of little help. Battling the remnants of a bout of bronchitis as well as foul trouble, the usually sleek senior was a step slow all day. He finished with only seven points—including just three free throws in the second half—and only one rebound, his least productive game since his sophomore season.

The Wolverines also had to overcome the absence of Kirk Taylor, who had been their third guard until he suffered a season-ending knee injury eight days earlier in Minnesota. Briefly, Frieder had tried sophomore Demetrius Calip and freshman Rob Pelinka in his place. Both were burned badly on defense. Meanwhile, Robinson was playing with a partially torn ligament in his right thumb, Higgins was playing despite a slight hamstring pull, and Vaught and Griffin were battling bad colds.

Even so, when Robinson—who would end with 24 points—hit two foul shots with 2:11 left, Michigan owned a 70–69 lead. And when Higgins drilled a 3-pointer with 1:10 remaining, Michigan was up 75–71. Even after Edwards made two free throws, the Wolverines had a 75–73 lead and the ball, with just 54 seconds remaining.

They had it won.

All they had to do was run off as much of the 45-second clock as they could, which they did. All they had to do was get a good shot late in that segment, which they did. All they had to do was knock down that shot, or if it missed, play nine or 10 seconds of good enough defense to keep Indiana from getting one good, last shot.

The Wolverines did almost all of those things. Almost. They ran the clock

The Michigan Wolverines can't believe they've just been beaten by Jay Edwards' last-second 3-pointer. As coach Bill Frieder stands with his hands on his hips, assistant coach Steve Fisher argues with an official.

Indiana's Jamal Meeks jumps for joy and Jay Edwards is buried beneath happy Hoosiers, while in the background a shocked Loy Vaught still can't believe the Hoosiers beat the Wolverines for a second time.

down. Higgins started to penetrate, drew the defense to him, and passed off to the 6–7 Rice, who had posted up 6–6 Brian Sloan near the baseline, just to the right of the paint.

As Frieder said later, "We got the ball to our All-American on the block. You can't do any better than that. He makes that shot and it doesn't matter what Indiana does."

But Rice, the deadliest shooter in Michigan history, put up a soft five-footer that rolled around the rim and fell off. Indiana freshman Eric Anderson grabbed it, fed Jones, and . . .

Indiana 76, Michigan 75.

Indiana, winner of two games against Michigan by a total of two points, now had a virtual lock on the Big Ten title. Even if the Wolverines couldn't have caught the Hoosiers themselves, they needed to beat them in order to give second-place Illinois, 8–4, a chance to overtake them. But now it was the Hoosiers in first place in the Big Ten, ranked ninth in the country, and headed upward after a 3–4 start. And it was Michigan in third place in the Big Ten, ranked 13th and headed down after winning its first 11 games.

"We may have played better than I thought we could play," Knight said after the game. "I'm not sure Michigan didn't play quite a bit better than Michigan played in Ann Arbor. I think they're awfully good, and I'm no great Michigan fan."

Said Frieder: "I have no complaints about my basketball team. They played their butts off and gave a great effort, especially since we've had so much ill-ness and injury that we haven't had a good practice all week."

Maybe Frieder didn't have any complaints. But assistant coach Steve Fisher did. After the game, he walked across the Michigan lockerroom, where players were angrily throwing their shoes and uniforms on the floor. "We got cheated," said one. "The refs were intimidated by Bobby Knight," said another.

Fisher bent down and whispered in Rice's ear.

"Glen, you're better than that," he told the senior forward and co-captain. "You've got to go out there thinking you're the best. You've got to think you can't be stopped. No matter if you're sick or hurt, you've got to just go out there and give your best effort. You've got to suck it up and go out there and kick some butt."

At first, Rice recalled later, "I was leaning toward denying it. But I knew he was right. He could see it. He was watching."

For a few moments, the Wolverines just sat there. Then something unusual happened. Rice, who vastly preferred to let his actions do his talking, spoke up.

"It was kind of like the 'big wow,'" said Griffin. "It was an inspiring speech. Glen's kind of quiet. That's why it had the greatest impact."

Rice's "speech" was hardly long enough to qualify for that title. But its impact was far greater than its length.

"Screw this," Rice told his teammates. "I'm tired of this. I'm tired of losing games we should win. We aren't losing anymore. We are going to win the rest of our games, and we are going to win all our games in the tournament, and we are going to be national champs. We are going on a mission, a mission to shock the world."

Sean Higgins clapped his hands together. "Yeah, baby, that's right," he said. "We are on a mission from here on out."

When the Wolverines returned to Ann Arbor that evening, Frieder gave his managers an assignment.

They went into the Michigan lockerroom and headed for the door of equipment manager Bob Bland. On that door was a picture of the Big Ten trophy, over which had been placed strips of paper, each one inscribed with one of Michigan's Big Ten games. One of Frieder's limitless motivational ploys, the idea had been to uncover a little more of the championship with each Wolverine win, until finally the Big Ten trophy would come into view—and grasp.

Now, managers took the Big Ten "puzzle" down. In its place, they put a picture of the NCAA Tournament trophy. Over it, they placed 12 strips of paper: one for each of Michigan's six remaining regular season games, and one for each of the six games it would take for the Wolverines to win the national championship.

"The Mission" had begun.

A Season on the Brink

Glen Rice and his Michigan teammates may have been disheartened by their second loss to Indiana, but they were no more disheartened than Bill Frieder and Steve Fisher.

Although the basic psychology of coaching kept them from proclaiming it publicly, both Frieder and Fisher had entered the 1988–89 season with high hopes. This was Frieder's ninth team as Michigan head coach and the 16th he had been involved with as either head or assistant coach. On paper at least, Frieder knew it should be his best team since the 1985–86 squad, which had gone 28–5 and had won a second straight Big Ten championship. In fact, Frieder knew this just might be his best team ever. The Wolverines returned seven of the top eight players from a squad that had gone 26–8 in 1987–88, finishing second in the Big Ten and 10th in the country. Michigan had led the nation in field goal percentage (54.6 percent), had led the Big Ten in scoring margin, and had advanced to the Sweet 16 of the NCAA Tournament. The team Frieder would field for 1988–89 would have just about everything a college coach dreams of: size, depth, experience, and skilled players.

Leading the list was Glen Rice, a 6–7 senior forward from Flint, Michigan. As a junior, Rice led the Big Ten in scoring with a 22.9 average. He could score on solid post-up moves inside or blister the nets from 3-point range, and he could also rebound with the Big Ten's best. Shy and unassuming, except around his closest friends off the court, Rice was a bona fide pre-season All-America on it.

Joining him up front were 6–8 senior Mark Hughes and a pair of juniors, 6–10 Terry Mills and 6–9 Loy Vaught. Hughes, a burly banger from Muskegon, Michigan, was a steady, heady player who would serve along with Rice as a co-captain. Bright and personable, he was an excellent liaison between the coaches and players off court. On the floor, he excelled at defense and rebounding, and he could score when that was needed.

8

Bill Frieder's final Michigan team had lots of weapons, beginning with All-American Glen Rice.

Mills, from Romulus, Michigan, had been ranked alongside North Carolina's J. R. Reid as the nation's two best players coming out of high school. Mills had missed his freshman season due to Proposition 48, and during his sophomore year some fans were perturbed when he wasn't as dominant as they had expected. Still, he had averaged 12.2 points and 6.4 rebounds, and had finished third in the Big Ten in blocked shots. Mills' sensitive nature and quick wit belied a body that looked big and mean. Actually, he needed to get a little meaner to be truly successful in the rugged Big Ten, but there was no doubt he had all the skills—including phenomenal passing ability—to become one of the country's best big men.

Vaught, from East Grand Rapids, Michigan, had the kind of lean, muscular body that seemed designed for basketball. He had sat out his first season as a redshirt, then gained more and more playing time the next two seasons. Like Mills, Vaught needed to get meaner and more consistent. But when he was on his game, Vaught could be a spectacular player. He could soar for rebounds and slam dunks, and he had made 62.1 percent of his field goal tries as a sophomore.

For backup help along the frontline, Michigan had: J. P. Oosterbaan, a beefy, 6–11 redshirt junior who was an exceptional student of the game; Chris Seter, a 6–9 redshirt freshman; and a pair of true freshmen, 7–0 Eric Riley and 6–7 James Voskuil. As the 1988–89 season progressed, it would turn out that Seter would be sidelined for the entire year by an arm injury, and Riley and Voskuil would both be redshirted. But so deep were the Wolverines that their absence was never really noticed.

In the backcourt, Michigan had lost the services of All-American Gary Grant, who had rewritten much of the Wolverines' record book during four years as a starter. But there was plenty of talent returning, led by 6–2 junior Rumeal Robinson. A power-packed lead guard in the mold of the Detroit Pistons' Vinnie Johnson, Robinson combined breathtaking leaping ability with phenomenal upper body strength. His average of 4.8 assists was the best of any returning Big Ten guard. Like Mills, Robinson had been rated among the country's top five players as a high school senior, but had to sit out his freshman year under Proposition 48. A tireless worker, he had improved his outside shooting greatly, and began his junior year poised on the brink of stardom.

To complement Robinson, the Wolverines had: 6–9 sophomore Sean Higgins, another high school All-America who could shoot, handle the ball, and rebound; 6–7 redshirt junior Mike Griffin, an intelligent player and a defensive specialist; 6–4 sophomore Kirk Taylor, a solid all-around player who seemed to lack only experience; 6–1 sophomore Demetrius Calip, a cat-quick point guard; and 6–5 freshman Rob Pelinka, a 3-point specialist from suburban Chicago.

It was a team which seemed to have virtually everything, including versatility. If the need arose, Higgins and Griffin could swing between the front-

Sophomore guard Rumeal Robinson gave the Wolverines some headaches, but he also supplied plenty of instant offense.

court and backcourt, making Michigan's depth even greater. Frieder insisted that backcourt inexperience would be a problem because Robinson was the only guard who had played a great deal the previous year. But it seemed quite possible that once some of the other guards saw more action that deficiency would be easily remedied. As Frieder and Fisher sized up their team, they had to like what they saw.

Fisher was beginning his seventh year as Frieder's apprentice. For three years before that, he had been an assistant at Western Michigan. Before that, he had been a highly successful head coach for eight years at Rich East, a suburban high school south of Chicago. As Frieder's unofficial top assistant, Fisher was involved in virtually all aspects of the program, particularly running practices, formulating strategy, and, to a lesser extent, recruiting. He knew the team well and, like Frieder, felt it might be their best Michigan team yet.

Besides their omnipresent competitive natures, both men had personal reasons that had them hoping the 1988–89 year would be a banner season.

Fisher would turn 44 in March. Although he loved Michigan and realized he had one of the best assistants' jobs in America, he had decided it was time for him to try for a job as a Division I head coach. In the fall, before the season began, he had discussed it with his wife, Angie. They had decided he would begin a concerted two-year effort to land a head coaching job. Fisher approached Bo Schembechler, Michigan athletic director and football coach, and explained his situation. Schembechler promised to provide Fisher with a reference.

For Frieder, 1988–89 promised to be a season on the brink. Heading into fall practice, he knew that this could either be a year when he silenced his critics or a year when those critics' voices would grow stronger. Although Frieder had won nearly three-fourths of his games since succeeding Johnny Orr as Michigan coach in 1980–81, he hadn't been able to win over the fans or the media to the same degree. Even though he began the season with five straight 20-win seasons, four consecutive trips to the NCAA Tournament, two Big Ten championships, and a NIT title, Frieder wasn't on the firmest footing with the Michigan faithful.

Part of Frieder's problem was that he had never been able to match his regular-season success in the all-important NCAA Tournament, a surefire source of fuel for eager critics. Partly because of that, Frieder had been unable to shake his image as a great recruiter but only average bench coach. And the rest of Frieder's image—which had been slipping since he was named National Coach of the Year in 1985—took a battering during the 1987–88 season.

In October 1987, Dallas Mavericks' forward Roy Tarpley, a former Michigan star, revealed he had undergone treatment for cocaine and alcohol problems. A few days later, the *Ann Arbor News*, quoting unidentified sources close to the Wolverines, reported that Tarpley had failed at least one and perhaps three drug tests during his junior and senior years at Michigan without being suspended. Columnists and editorial writers criticized Frieder for not having dealt with Tarpley's problem more forcefully.

Then in January, Higgins, a star freshman swingman who was Frieder's latest recruiting prize, was declared academically ineligible along with fellow frosh Calip. Although they were the first players Frieder had ever lost to grade problems, the coach was again criticized: basketball zealots ripped him for losing a key player and those more concerned with academics chided him for letting his team's studies slip.

In January 1988, Michigan was en route to chalking up a very impressive 120–103 homecourt victory over a very good Iowa team when Frieder encountered another problem. Enraged by an official's failure to call a technical foul against Iowa's Ed Horton just before halftime, Frieder stormed off the court at the half, shouting over his shoulder at the official. As he approached the Crisler Arena tunnel, Frieder turned to find a television camera thrust close to his face. Looking more like a madman than anyone with a 35-point lead has a right to, Frieder swiped at the camera with one arm, knocking it out of his way.

Some observers mistakenly thought Frieder had pushed the cameraman, and some newspaper stories the next day reported as much. Joe Falls, sports editor of the *Detroit News*, wrote a column criticizing Frieder for such behavior. Frieder compounded the problem when, during the press conference following the Wolverines' next game, he tried to convince Falls that what he had written was wrong. As the exchange between the two men grew somewhat heated, it was obvious to many of the reporters in the room that Frieder was digging himself into a hole with Falls, one of the most powerful sportswriters in the state.

Then came the Texas fiasco.

While Michigan was preparing to open NCAA play in mid-March, the *Detroit News* reported that Frieder had been approached by the University of Texas about its head coaching position. One week later, an Associated Press story quoted Texas athletic director DeLoss Dodds as saying that Frieder had approached Texas about the job, not the other way around. When it became known that the *Detroit News'* original story had been prompted by what Frieder had regarded as an off-the-record comment, some columnists and commentators suggested that Frieder had planted the story in an effort to gain sympathy—and perhaps a fatter contract—when he would subsequently appear to remain faithful to Michigan. When Frieder steadfastly refused to discuss the matter, saying to do so was only bound to make someone look bad, some columnists—especially Falls and Mick McCabe of the *Detroit Free Press*—ripped him for being dishonest. That incident rankled Schembechler, who was appointed athletic director shortly afterwards. Although few people outside the Michigan athletic department knew it at the time, Schembechler

J.P. Oosterbaan was a solid backup player who knew the game so well that teammates valued his advice highly.

was no fan of Frieder. When the veteran football coach succeeded longtime athletic director Don Canham in the summer of 1988, Frieder not only lost a trusted ally but acquired in his place a skeptical new boss.

In the meantime, Frieder didn't even have his customary recruiting success to fall back on. In fact, he had endured one of his leanest recruiting years ever. Cross-state rival Jud Heathcote of Michigan State snapped up Matt Steigenga, the state's Mr. Basketball and a player Frieder had pursued for years, plus Michigan's four other top high school seniors. Frieder signed three players, but for the first time in several years he failed to sign even one blue-chip prospect.

A solid season in 1988–89 could go a long way toward easing Frieder's problems. But anything less than a very successful season might only compound them. Expectations were very high. Most pre-season magazines rated Michigan among their top five teams, and some rated it number one. The 1988–89 season had the potential to be a breakthrough year for Frieder. *Inside Sports* picked the Wolverines to win it all, and used a story on Frieder as its main college preview story. Shortly after the season began, Frieder's autobiography, *Basket Case,* was scheduled for publication. Frieder hoped his book and his team would help him regain some lost popularity. But by the time Jay Edwards' buzzer-beating bomb knocked Michigan out of the Big Ten title chase, that had not happened. If anything, Frieder was on shakier ground than before. So when Frieder heard Glen Rice's uncharacteristic urging about going on "a mission," he was only too glad to embrace the crusade. Frieder was already on a mission, and the only way to accomplish it was by winning.

Mike Griffin could score, but his main contributions came at the defensive end.

Three to Get Ready

For the Michigan Wolverines, the week following the Indiana game would be crucial. They would play three games in a five-day span, all against teams they would be favored to beat. It promised to be a grueling stretch, but it also promised a chance to get things straight and to start building momentum for the NCAA Tournament.

The first obstacle was the Ohio State Buckeyes, ranked No. 20 in the country by the Associated Press.

On paper, Ohio State looked like fairly easy prey, especially since the Buckeyes had lost their best player, senior guard Jay Burson, to a career-threatening neck injury one week before. But the Buckeyes figured to have a few things going for them. They were playing at home, where Michigan hadn't won in the last two seasons. Burson would be sitting alongside the bench, and the appearance of the battered little guard, who had been outfitted with a bizarre-looking halo brace, was likely to get Ohio State and its fans—already the Big Ten's rowdiest—extra revved up. Also, the Buckeyes were battling for a NCAA Tournament berth. And if they needed any more incentive, the Wolverines had crushed them, 99–73, a month before in Ann Arbor. Bill Frieder had left his starters in that game long after it had been decided, and OSU coach Gary Williams noted then that "our players have long memories."

As it turned out, those memories were largely of Burson, who had not only run the Buckeye show from his point guard position but had also averaged 22 points in Big Ten play. Without him, the Buckeyes were destined to flounder their way out of a NCAA bid, losing their last seven games before rebounding to make a decent showing in the NIT. This game against Michigan was only their second game without Burson, and the Buckeyes were hopelessly outgunned. The Wolverines broke the game open midway through the first half, putting together a 22–7 run over an eight-minute stretch. They went

Rumeal Robinson had played well against Ohio State even when the Buckeyes had Jay Burson in their lineup. Without Burson, OSU was no match for Robinson and the Wolverines.

on to record an 89–72 rout that ended a 14-game OSU homecourt winning streak.

Although the disarray of the Burson-less Buckeyes certainly played a large role in Michigan's win and made it difficult to assess just how well the Wolverines had really played, there were undeniably some positive signs for Michigan.

Rice reverted to his explosive form, scoring 30 points on 11-of-21 field goal tries, including four slam dunks and two 3-pointers. He was more active on the boards and defensively, grabbing six rebounds, notching three steals, and holding Buckeyes senior forward Jerry Francis, who had been averaging 12.6 points, to a mere two.

"I'm not a lot better," Rice said of his bronchitis, an illness that had dogged him throughout his Michigan career. "But I was moving a lot better than I did in the last game. I just put in my mind that I wasn't sick. I think the more I can do that, the better I can play."

Terry Mills, whose total of seven rebounds in Michigan's previous three games had been called "ridiculous" by Frieder, matched that total against OSU, and added 12 points. Sean Higgins scored only four points but had an unusually high five assists. Loy Vaught, who led the nation in field goal percentage for much of the season, scored 15 points on 6-of-7 fielders and also ripped down a game-high 12 rebounds.

"This was a very big game," Vaught said. "They hadn't been beaten here in some time and we were coming off that tough, tough Indiana loss. We've been talking ever since then of our mission. We have aspirations of going 12–0 from here on out, and that had to begin here."

Among the brightest signs for Michigan was the play of point guard Rumeal Robinson, who sometimes had thrown the Wolverine offense out of sync by trying to do too much himself. Against the Buckeyes, Robinson turned in a fine all-around game with 16 points, nine assists, and five rebounds.

"I think Rumeal is feeling more comfortable with his role," said OSU coach Williams, who as coach at Boston College had followed Robinson throughout his high school career at Cambridge, Massachusetts, Rindge and Latin. "By next year, he'll be one of the premier point guards in the country."

Two days later, the Wolverines were at home against the surprising Wisconsin Badgers, who brought a 16–7 record and six wins in their last eight Big Ten games into Crisler Arena.

The Badgers, sniffing their first shot at post-season play in 47 years, were both hot and rested. They had had a week to rest since their last game, when they had upset No. 10 Illinois by 20 points. They had upset Michigan the month before in Madison, and another win over the Wolverines would tie them with Michigan for fourth place in the Big Ten.

But the only upset destined to occur in Ann Arbor on this Saturday was

Demetrius Calip did more than lead cheers against Michigan State.

the feeling in Wisconsin coach Steve Yoder's stomach. Hitting 63.4 percent of their field goals—including 76.9 from 3-point land—the Wolverines demolished the Badgers, 92–70.

With Rice hitting 7-of-7 3-pointers and pouring in 38 points to pass Cazzie Russell as the No. 3 scorer in Michigan history, the Wolverines roared to a 46–23 lead with two minutes left in the first half. As the teams headed back onto the floor for the second half, Yoder, knowing his fate was sealed, paused for a moment as he passed Frieder. "Boy," he said, "you guys are playing great."

In his post-game press conference, Yoder elaborated. "Do you realize Michigan might have been the best team in the country today?" he asked. "Do you know how tough it is to stop two 6–8 guys (Rice and Sean Higgins) who are hitting 3-pointers? It's very tough. Give the credit to Michigan. They were great. Write it."

According to Robinson, Wisconsin's fate had been written on Rice's face early in the game.

"He had that smile," Robinson said, "and when he's smiling like that you know he's paying attention and is really into the game. It was a Glen Rice day. It was one of those days, just like in practice, where you just throw him the ball and he shoots it in."

Although Rice—who admitted, "That's as hot as I can remember being in a while"—was the prime attraction, he wasn't the whole Wolverine show. Robinson counted 11 points and 10 assists. Vaught had 12 points and 11 rebounds, and Higgins added 14 points.

"We just played an outstanding 17–18 minutes in the first half," Frieder said. "Who knows what would have happened if I hadn't gone to the bench?"

Said Wisconsin senior center Darin Schubring: "They shot unbelievably. Every time I blocked out and turned around, the ball was going through the net. And every time, it was hitting nothing but net."

Michigan's three games-in-five days trial was to end with a Monday night game at Michigan State that shaped up as a special confrontation. Not only would the intrastate rivalry be televised on ESPN, but because the Spartans were scheduled to move into a new arena in 1989, it would be the final Michigan-MSU game ever played in venerable Jenison Field House.

At only 13–11 overall and just 4–10 in the Big Ten, the youthful and small Spartans were struggling. But over the years, the Michigan-MSU rivalry had been one to which the adage about throwing records out the window truly applied. In these games, one never knew what to expect. It was likely to be a stern test for the Wolverines.

The Spartans stunned Michigan by making the first three baskets of the game, quickly prompting Frieder to burn a timeout. Later in the half, three more unanswered baskets gave MSU a 32–27 lead with 3:56 remaining.

But then Demetrius Calip, who spelled Robinson for the final 6:21 of the half, sparked a Michigan surge. He hit two jumpers, dished off to Mills for a two-hand slam, and set the stage for a Vaught tip-in by driving to the hoop as the clock wound down. Michigan scored the final 11 points of the half, then netted the first five of the second half. Then the Wolverines finished the Spartans off, outshooting them 67–24 percent after intermission, holding MSU to just 20 second-half points, and walking away from Jenison with a 79–52 victory.

Balance was a key for Michigan. MSU used all kinds of gimmick defenses to hold Rice, who had been averaging 26.1 points, to only nine. So the Wolverines decided to use Rice primarily as a decoy. Nine other Wolverines got into the scoring column, led by Vaught's 16 points.

"You can't lead the nation in field goal percentage like we are without unselfish play. I don't deserve the credit, but the kids do," Frieder told reporters after the game. "Glen wasn't concerned about scoring 25 points tonight, just winning the ball game. He became a decoy and a screener, setting up the inside people. And that's really something for an All-American scorer like Glen."

Rice, finally almost recovered from his bronchitis, seemed as proud of excelling in that role as he had been of pouring in the points in Michigan's two previous wins.

"They played great defense on me," he said. "Everywhere I went, they bumped me. But the coaches did a great job of preparing me for this game. Tonight I did things people didn't think I could do to get everyone involved."

As a result, the Wolverines were involved in a three-game winning streak. And now a full quarter of the NCAA puzzle on equipment manager Bob Bland's door was visible.

Great Expectations

One of the things that drives college basketball coaches crazy is the frequent difference between the way they see their teams and the way their teams are viewed by fans and the media. For Bill Frieder and his staff, this difference was never more noticeable than during the 1988–89 season.

Especially in late January, when the Wolverines dropped back-to-back Big Ten games to Wisconsin and Indiana.

Michigan had started its season as strongly as many observers had predicted, beating Vanderbilt, Memphis State, and Oklahoma to win the championship of the Maui Classic in Hawaii. The Wolverines returned home to win eight more games, running their season-opening win streak to 11 games and rising to a No. 2 ranking. Michigan lost that with an embarrassing upset loss to Division II Alaska-Anchorage, but righted itself to begin pursuit of the Big Ten title with homecourt wins over Northwestern and Minnesota. Then the Wolverines, facing their first crucial conference challenge, were pounded at Illinois, 96–84. That loss was disappointing, but not overly surprising or discouraging; after all, in nine seasons as Michigan's head coach, Frieder had never won in Champaign.

But then after a home victory over Ohio State, the Wolverines were upset by the Wisconsin Badgers, 71–68, at Madison. Two days later, Indiana came to Ann Arbor for an ESPN Monday night game.

Among Michigan basketball fans, no rival is more hated than the Indiana Hoosiers, no conference coach more despised than Bob Knight—especially after 1984, when Knight and Frieder had a run-in that escalated into a long-running personal feud.

So it was that, with a national audience watching on TV on this Monday night in January, it became apparent that Frieder was in trouble with the Wolverine faithful. TV cameras zeroed in on a "Fire Frieder" sign in the crowd.

And when Frieder's name was called during pre-game introductions, the capacity Crisler Arena crowd booed him just as lustily as the hated Knight. "That hurt, that really hurt," Frieder admitted a few weeks later. "After a tough loss against Wisconsin, we needed our fans' support. I think it bothered the team and distracted them a little bit early. I was shocked. That was one of the things that registered."

When the game ended with Indiana winning, 71–70, as Michigan missed two shots in the final seconds, many Wolverine fans were stunned and angry. Their team, picked to contend for the conference crown, suddenly had a mediocre 3–3 Big Ten record. The race was only one-third of the way over, but already the Wolverines had pretty much fallen out of it.

Much of the media readily joined in on the increasingly popular sport of Michigan-bashing.

Ann Arbor News columnist Chris McCosky found fault with the Wolverines at both ends of the floor: "Bill Frieder blamed his team's offensive breakdowns on his guards. That's too easy. There's more to it than that. It's very difficult for a guard to distribute the ball inside when all the inside players keep floating out to the perimeter . . . (and) Michigan tends to play heavy-footed, half-hearted defense."

Other scribes were even harsher. John Harris, columnist for the *St. Petersburg Times*, wrote: "Talent abounds at Michigan, at every position but coach . . . the Michigan basketball team has enough McDonald's All-Americans to create a new fast-food venue . . . but most of all, they lack a coach . . . (Frieder is) a nice enough man who can't seem to get his players to play to their full potential . . . coaches like Bobby Knight and Gary Williams have gilded their records at the expense of the Wolverines."

Never mind that when those words were written, Knight's lifetime record against Frieder was only 9–8 and Williams' career mark vs. Frieder was 2–3. Like a self-fulfilling prophecy, the rap on Frieder had taken on a life of its own.

After the season was over, Fisher said: "It just seemed like people went from talking about . . . 'they're playing well, they're also playing hard and together,' to 'they're a group of talented individuals but to blend together and do what it really takes to win, they don't do it and the coaching is not as good as it should be.' I felt like too many people were too quick to jump off a boat that maybe didn't even have much of a leak. I felt that Bill got too much blame during that stretch that wasn't merited or warranted, and the team, I also felt, was perceived a little too harshly. I don't think it was demoralizing to the players, although maybe it made them mad. Our kids, like most, have big egos. They think they're good. It doesn't matter what you say, they still think they're good."

As the Wolverines headed into the final three games of the regular season, many fans and much of the media had written them off. But the players and

Glen Rice and Bill Frieder always felt they were part of an outstanding team; Michigan fans didn't always agree.

Rumeal Robinson was one reason Iowa's Ed Horton said Michigan was "like a young NBA team."

coaches—and some other knowledgeable observers—still thought they were pretty good. After Michigan dismantled MSU, Terry Mills said: "We've heard all the criticisms and we're going to try and shut up the critics. It took us a long time to get our chemistry, but we've got it now and we're going to be a tough team to beat."

MSU coach Jud Heathcote thought Mills might just be right. "I think they're a definite contender for the Final Four," he said. "They have awesome talent." Of the Big Ten's top four teams of Indiana, Illinois, Michigan, and Iowa, Heathcote said, "Maybe the most talented would be Michigan because of its size inside, ability to shoot and pass so well, and they're playing very good defense right now."

When the No. 11 Iowa Hawkeyes came to Ann Arbor a few days later, the No. 10 Wolverines backed up those words. Notching seven steals, forcing 24 turnovers, and holding Iowa to 33 first-half points, Michigan raced to a 119–96 romp. True, the Hawkeyes had played without injured star guard B.J. Armstrong. Still, the Wolverines were impressive. They hit 62.8 percent of their shots to boost their nation-leading field goal percentage even higher. Rice burned the nets for 33 points, Robinson had 22 points and 10 assists, and Mills and Vaught added 18 points apiece.

"If Indiana's the champion of this league," said Iowa coach Tom Davis, "how far behind is Michigan? Two points, and maybe they're even better right now. It's so unbelievable that people can be critical of a program like this for underachieving. I recognize that Michigan is a very, very good basketball team right now and I look for them to make a very strong tournament run."

Said Iowa senior Ed Horton: "Michigan is a NBA-type team. They're a young pro team and they're ready for the tournament."

Undeniably Rumeal

One reason the Michigan Wolverines were rolling again was Rumeal Robinson. "We're playing much better right now, and the main reason we are is the play of Rumeal. He's becoming a floor leader," said Bill Frieder. Iowa coach Tom Davis was certainly convinced. "Michigan has a lot of great players," he said, "but I think Rumeal Robinson is really their key." Frieder had expected that would be the case one day, ever since he convinced Robinson to sign with Michigan. But getting to that point hadn't been easy.

During practice one day midway through the season, Frieder stood at Crisler Arena's center court, toe-to-toe with his junior guard. Frieder was berating Robinson, and he wasn't doing it quietly. He was yelling, his face thrust right into Robinson's. Finally, Frieder finished making his technical points. Then he screamed at Robinson: "Do you know why I'm doing this? Do you know why I'm yelling at you? Because I want to make you a great basketball player, that's why."

Robinson thrust his face right back into Frieder's. "I'm already a great player," he snarled.

If Glen Rice was the heart of Michigan's basketball team, Rumeal Robinson was its soul. Rice's shooting and boundless love of the game may have been inspirational, but Robinson's fierce determination and never-say-die attitude were positively uplifting. Steve Fisher once summed up Robinson in one neat phrase: "Rumeal simply won't be denied." Fisher was right. If one word could sum up a person, the word "determination" would do it for Robinson. He was a young man who simply would not admit defeat, no matter what the odds.

One day during the summer before his freshman season, the 6–2 Robinson was playing in a pickup game, along with several current and former Wolverines. A missed shot bounced toward the middle of the paint. Robinson snared the rebound, landing with his back to the basket. In the next motion, he rose

An extraordinary leaper, Rumeal Robinson could venture where few guards dared go.

upward, up and over the 6–11 defender between him and the basket. His back still to the hoop, he brought the ball up in front of him, lifting it with both hands, then throwing the ball down behind his head for a slam dunk. During the Wolverine's NCAA Tournament win over North Carolina, the 195-pound Robinson, who had a body like Rambo, found himself battling 6–10, 235-pound Scott Williams for a loose ball. First, Robinson had soared up to snatch the ball away from Williams. Then after Williams knocked it loose and grabbed it back, Robinson reached—once, twice, three times—and finally, with a sudden burst of strength, tore the ball right out of Williams' hands.

"He is fiercely proud," said Fisher. "Maybe even more competitive than proud. Maybe a little bit stubborn, but that stubborn streak has gotten him where he is. He always thinks 'I can do it.'"

Rumeal Robinson simply would not let the world defeat him, no matter how hard it tried.

And God knows, it had tried.

Robinson was six years old when he and his mother left their native Jamaica to move to the Boston area. He was nine when his mother abandoned him, leaving him to spend his nights going from door-to-door, staying a night or two at a time with various friends. Workers at a Cambridge community center pointed him out to Helen Ford, who remembered him from a youth football league. They talked for a while, and then she said, "Why don't you come home with me?" He did, and soon afterward Helen and Louis Ford—who already had six children—adopted him.

Robinson treasured his adopted family. A reporter once asked him if he considered himself lucky to have received the second chance the Fords had given him. "Not a second chance," Robinson corrected. "My only chance. My family has really helped. They're responsible for a lot of things. I always respected them and didn't want any bad things said about them because of me."

He needn't have worried. As he grew, Robinson developed into a tremendous basketball player and a better-than-average student. By the time he was a senior at Cambridge Rindge and Latin, the same school that had produced New York Knicks star Patrick Ewing, Robinson was rated alongside his friend, Rex Chapman, as the two best high school guards in the country. Robinson averaged 18.5 points, 10.4 rebounds, and 11 assists—a triple-double *average*—for his senior season. Recruited by everybody, he signed with Michigan, then was named along with future teammate Terry Mills to the McDonald's All-American Team. Robinson led Rindge & Latin to the Massachusetts state title, and gave his championship ring to his adopted father, Louis Ford. He was selected to play in that summer's Olympic Festival, a training ground for Olympic hopefuls.

Then the bottom fell out. Robinson finally encountered an obstacle he couldn't overcome. He couldn't get a high enough score on college entrance examinations to satisfy the requirements of the NCAA's new Proposition 48 rule, just going into effect that year. His high school grades had been more than enough to meet half of the requirements, but without the test scores Rumeal Robinson would be ineligible to play or practice as a freshman. He could still accept Michigan's scholarship, but he would have to forfeit his first year of eligibility. Fellow freshman Terry Mills suffered the same fate.

It was a terrible blow to Robinson, who suffered from a learning disability that made it hard for him to read. Because of that disability, college figured to be a real challenge to Robinson, even under the best of circumstances. Now he would not only have to adjust to college, he'd have to do it carrying the stigma of Proposition 48, and without the familiar comforts of basketball to fall back on. But Mrs. Ford said, "This could be a blessing in disguise. It will give him a chance to adjust to school and his schoolwork." And that's the way Robinson approached it. He tape-recorded his lectures and listened to the tapes over and over. He saw a tutor. And on an almost daily basis, he got extra tutoring help from Frieder's wife Janice, who had specialized in learning disabilities a few years earlier as a teacher consultant. He watched basketball from a distance, spending hours practicing his outside shooting and working with Mills. Although he could already bench-press 235 pounds, he continued to lift weights. At Michigan's home games, he and Mills sat near midcourt, watching and waiting. "There's a lot you can learn just by watching, and I'm trying to do that," Robinson said. But it was a painful process. Watching Michigan fatten up on its annual December home schedule, Robinson fidgeted and said, "I hope we play better teams than this next year." Off the court, he was stung by having people assume that his Proposition 48 distinction meant that he was dumb. Frieder placed Robinson and Mills off-limits to the media, but as the two biggest names to fall victim to Prop 48, they remained prime targets for inquiring minds. At one point, a newspaper reporter climbed through their dorm window, attempting to get an interview.

Robinson and Mills may have been out of sight on the basketball floor, but they were never out of mind where the media and basketball fans were concerned. There was pressure on them, not the least being that both players knew that their performances would go a long way toward deciding whether Michigan would accept more Prop 48 athletes in the future. Both players met the academic challenge, especially Robinson. When his freshman year ended, Rumeal Robinson had completed 38 hours of classroom credits—a heavy load for any freshman—with a 2.4 grade point average. "Rumeal is a very bright, insightful kid," said Colleen Fairbanks, his tutor that year. "He's done very well because he's very conscientious. He takes care of business." In the next two years, Robinson would continue to take care of business, on and off the court. He would begin his senior season on schedule to finish his degree early; this young man who had been labeled an academic risk would finish his Michigan career taking extra, perhaps graduate-level, classes. And never would he take a swipe at the rule that had sidelined him. Instead, he would

As his junior year progressed, Rumeal Robinson made the transition from off-guard to point guard.

Rumeal Robinson wasn't one to be deterred by larger opponents.

talk about how valuable that first year had been to him, how it had helped him grow and adjust, both academically and socially. "I wasn't a basketball star anymore, so I had the time to meet a lot of people and make a lot of friends I wouldn't have otherwise," he pointed out.

The Robinson those friends got to know was a special person. Quiet and soft-spoken, he was a little bit the loner, usually serious, sometimes moody. When other players were partying or going out and enjoying their celebrity status, Robinson was likely to be at home studying, talking long distance to his family, or relaxing with his favorite hobby: drawing. Art was an area where Robinson was nearly as gifted as basketball. While in high school, he had been offered a scholarship to the Boston School of Fine Arts and at Michigan art professors who saw his work were impressed. After a particularly tough game, Robinson might sit for hours at his drawing table, where he would get away from things by sketching, sometimes accompanying his sketches with brief poems. "Someday I'd like to own a gallery, a place that could encourage young kids with talent for art," he said.

In the meantime, there was basketball business to be taken care of. Robinson would take care of it with the same dogged determination he applied to his studies. In practice before his sophomore season, he strained ligaments in his right thumb. He would play with the injury, the kind that tended to reappear, for the next two seasons. In the summer between his sophomore and junior seasons, be broke a bone in his foot but missed almost no practice time because of it. As a sophomore, he learned to complement Gary Grant as the off-guard. Then as a junior, he made the transition to point guard.

Robinson struggled at times, as almost all new college players do. But he improved steadily, occasionally showing flashes of brilliance. Anyone who saw him play as a senior in high school and then as a sophomore in college could tell that the year away from competition had taken its toll. But Robinson never complained about it; he just kept working stoically. He was naturally persistent, a quality the Ford family had nurtured. Robinson remembered the time during junior high school, when he was named to play in an all-star football game Thanksgiving weekend. Robinson hated being cold, and he told Louis Ford he didn't want to play. "I thought he was going to die," Robinson said later. "He told me that in life you must always finish whatever you start. There was no way he was going to let me out of it, and that always stuck with me." That attitude proved to be a major asset to Robinson, both on and off the court. "It just comes back to self-discipline," he said. "You have to have something to shoot for and you don't need excuses. If you want to do something, just do it. Don't make excuses. Just do it."

During Michigan's national championship season, that phrase —"Just do it"—would become almost as much a slogan as the team's "mission." Robinson spoke it early in the fall, when some players reported to practice in less than peak condition, and made excuses about why they weren't in better shape.

Robinson fixed them with his no-nonsense expression. "I don't want to hear it," he said. "Just do it."

Robinson was especially determined that season. By most standards, his sophomore averages of 9.7 points and 4.8 assists would have been judged as very good for a player who was in his first year of Big Ten competition, especially one who had sat out the previous year. But to Robinson, they had been disappointing. So was Michigan's third-round exit from the NCAA Tournament. That 78–69 loss to North Carolina came despite a tremendous effort by Robinson, who scored a career-high 29 points and almost singlehandedly kept Michigan in the game. Disappointing, too, was what happened over the next summer—or, more accurately, what didn't happen. Robinson, who had played in Olympic Festivals the two previous years, was not invited to tryouts for the U.S. Olympic team, although teammates Grant, Mills, and Glen Rice were. Being left out hurt Robinson deeply, and made him only more determined than ever to prove himself. "People back home say I should've stayed in the East, that this style of ball isn't suited to me, that people out here don't appreciate what I can do," Robinson said. "But that's not the point. If people out here don't appreciate me, it's because I haven't played well enough to make them appreciate me. I guess I'm just going to have to show them more this year."

At times, Robinson showed them plenty. An astounding leaper, he could venture where few 6–2 guards feared to soar—and with his equally impressive upper-body strength, he could go right up against the giants he found waiting for him. Several times he did what teammate Loy Vaught said he most loved to watch: "When he goes up and blocks a shot, but instead of just blocking it, grabs it with both hands and hangs on." Meanwhile, the long hours of working on his outside and free throw shooting were paying off. As a junior, he was more consistent in both areas, and he had increased his range to become a 3-point threat.

But college basketball wasn't just one long, upward spiral for Robinson. In high school, he had always been the go-to man, the guy who made things happen. As Michigan's point guard, he would be expected to be more of a set-up man, less an individual creator. As the Wolverines' most experienced guard, he would have to lead the team both offensively and defensively. The Wolverines would need him on the floor as much as possible, meaning he would have to learn to pick his spots and give the ball up rather than forcing the action and drawing the charging fouls that had plagued him. He would have to learn to recognize changing defenses and change Michigan's offense accordingly. He would need to learn to yield to co-captains Rice and Mark Hughes in some things, but to stake his claim as leader on the floor.

Determined or not, these weren't easy adjustments for Robinson. Part of the problem was his innate stubbornness. Robinson was one of those people who rarely doubt themselves. He wasn't afraid to speak his mind, no matter

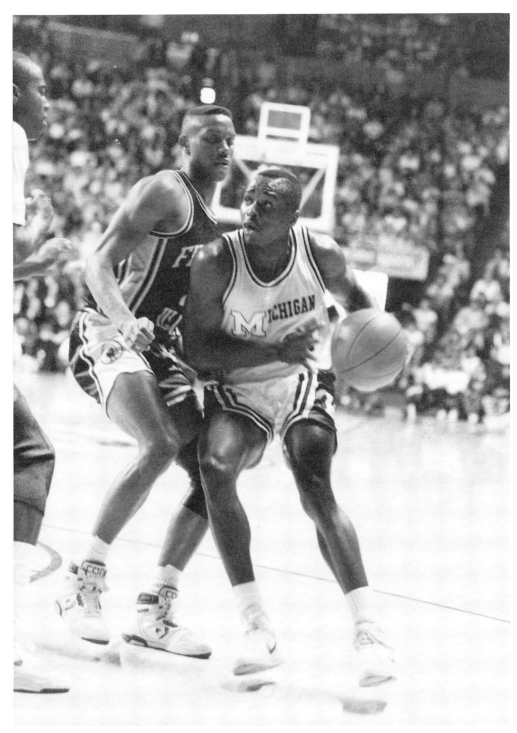

Rumeal Robinson's philosophy was simple: "If you want to do something, don't make excuses. Just do it."

Rumeal Robinson turned down an art scholarship to play in Ann Arbor. He says he'd like to open a gallery for young artists to encourage them to develop their skills. (Photo by: Colleen Fitzgerald)

who he was talking to or what he was talking about. After Robinson had played fairly poorly against Eastern Michigan, Frieder told reporters that EMU sophomore guard Lorenzo Neely had outplayed Robinson. When reporters relayed Frieder's assessment to Robinson, he said, "He can think whatever he wants. We won, didn't we? If he had outplayed me, they would've won." After the season, during the week between the national championship game and the hiring of Steve Fisher, Robinson told *Sports Illustrated* that Bo Schembechler was delaying his decision because "he just wants everyone to know that Michigan football is bigger than Michigan basketball." A friend told Robinson he should be careful of making such statements. "What if Bo called you in and asked you why you said that?" asked the friend. "I'd tell him because it was true, because I don't think he should think that way, and maybe he'd like to change," answered Robinson. As Steve Fisher said, such stubbornness was one reason Robinson was such an outstanding competitor. But the flip side was that it occasionally caused problems.

Another problem may have been Robinson's learning disability. As the season wore on, Michigan coaches grew frustrated over his seeming inability to recognize defensive changes and call for the offensive adjustments they necessitated. They didn't want to resort to hand signals or cue cards, as some programs did. They wanted Robinson to run the show. But they weren't pleased by the way things were going. Gradually, they began simplifying the offense, giving Robinson fewer options from which to choose. It was a decision that seemed to work; as the year continued, Robinson's decision-making seemed to get better and better.

Nevertheless, it had been an up-and-down season for Robinson. In the first two games of the Maui Classic, he played erratically, getting in frequent foul trouble. The steady play of Rice and the surprisingly solid showing of Kirk Taylor were the prime forces behind the Wolverines' wins over Vanderbilt and Memphis State. Then in the championship game against Oklahoma, Robinson was matched against Mookie Blaylock, a pre-season All-America. Although he eventually fouled out, the Michigan guard responded to the challenge brilliantly, scoring 20 points, handing off five assists, and notching two steals while limiting Blaylock to 11 points, five assists, and no steals. For most of December, Robinson continued to play well. But against the quick and scrappy guards of Alaska-Anchorage, he came up short, finishing with only nine points and four assists while committing five turnovers and four fouls. The Seawolves upset previously undefeated and No. 2 Michigan, 70–66. Coach Bill Frieder was so upset with Robinson's lackluster play that he didn't start him the next night against Holy Cross, marking only the second time since Robinson became eligible that he didn't start a game. Robinson's response: In only 23 minutes of action he scored eight points, had seven assists, grabbed four rebounds, and snatched four steals to help Michigan to a 100–63 victory. The next game, Robinson was back in the starting lineup and things were on an upswing again. Then came Michigan's January 21 game at Wisconsin. Robinson struggled to an eight-point, five-assist performance. But with nine seconds left and the Wolverines trailing, 69–68, he had two free throws and the chance to be the hero. He missed both foul shots, and the Badgers went on to post a 71–68 upset. Robinson, who hated to lose more than any of the Wolverines, who brooded even after wins if the team hadn't played well, was devastated. It was the kind of challenge that great players thrive on, and he had fallen short.

The next day, Robinson arrived at practice early. For the next few days, he came early every day, shooting 100 extra free throws each practice. He would not let the team down again, Robinson told himself and his teammates. The next time, he would be ready. He would not be denied.

Building Momentum?

On Thursday, March 10, Michigan continued to build tourney momentum by passing a pesky Northwestern team, 88–79, in Evanston.

This time, it was Mills' turn to step forward. The 6–11 junior scored only nine points, but he dazzled the Wildcats—and Northwestern coach Bill Foster—with his other skills. He handed out seven assists—including some deft no-look and wraparound passes—grabbed five rebounds and blocked five shots.

"He can really jump and he's very intimidating," said Foster. "His blocks are the kind that break your back. He could have blocked them with his elbow."

Just as impressive was Mills' passing, something he did as well as any big man in the country. It was the third time that season he had seven assists. That bumped his season total to 82, the same number as guard Phil Styles, Northwestern's assists leader. Said Bill Frieder: "Terry Mills, in the middle of the game when we were pulling away, was fantastic."

If Mills was fantastic, you'd have to create a new adjective for Glen Rice. He hit 11-of-19 shots for 26 points and grabbed a game-high nine rebounds. His point total pushed him past Gary Grant and made him the number two scorer in Michigan history with 2,244 career points. Only Mike McGee, with a seemingly unassailable career total of 2,439, ranked ahead of Rice.

The victory was Michigan's fifth straight and the Wolverines' ninth in the last 11. But there were still doubters. Sure, Michigan had won five straight. But take a closer look at those wins, they said. The Wolverines had beaten Ohio State, but so had everybody else since the Buckeyes had lost Jay Burson. Wisconsin? Michigan should have beaten the Badgers in Ann Arbor. Michigan State? The Spartans were hardly a powerhouse. Iowa? Michigan had beaten the Hawkeyes without B.J. Armstrong. Northwestern? The Wildcats were the Big Ten's perennial cellar dweller. What would happen when Michigan played a truly strong team? What would happen when the Wolverines ended their regular season with a home game against No. 4 Illinois?

In his nine seasons at Michigan, Bill Frieder had established a few traditions of which he was especially proud. One was that his Wolverines rarely fell victim to losing streaks. Another was that the Wolverines traditionally finished strongly, especially at home.

In 1986, the Big Ten race between Michigan and Indiana came down to the final game at Crisler Arena. The Wolverines, who had beaten the Hoosiers by only five points in Bloomington, blew them out of Crisler Arena, 83–52. In 1987, heavily favored Purdue was in position to clinch the outright Big Ten title by beating Michigan in the season final at Crisler. In West Lafayette, the Boilermakers had dispatched the Wolverines, 80–77. But at Crisler, on national television, Michigan handed Purdue a humiliating 104–68 defeat. In 1988, the Wolverines capped their year by hanging a 95–76 defeat on an Ohio State team that had beaten them in Columbus.

As they headed into the final regular season game of 1989, the Wolverines had plenty of incentive to record another trademark closing win. First, there was their mission, the first half of which was nearly complete. Second was the matter of avenging their earlier loss to the Fighting Illini. Then there was the matter of jockeying for position in the NCAA Tournament. A win over Illinois would virtually guarantee No. 8 Michigan a No. 2 seed. And if Indiana should lose its season finale at Iowa while Michigan won, there was a chance the NCAA tourney committee might even seed the Wolverines above the Hoosiers.

When Robinson scored Michigan's first three baskets to stake the Wolverines to a 7–2 lead, it seemed the Maize and Blue were en route to following their traditional season-ending script. But to some observers, Robinson's start was a bad omen. Throughout the year, Michigan had usually struggled when the powerful junior had tried to do too much himself and prospered when he concentrated on first getting his teammates involved.

Then there was Rice, who had played so well since the loss at Indiana. This was his final home game, and he was greeted with a thunderous standing ovation when he was introduced before the game along with members of his family. Standing at center court, he almost appeared dazed as he tried to fight back his tears. Onlookers who knew Rice well, who knew what a sensitive, shy young man he was, wondered whether the outpouring of affection would inspire him or throw him off his game.

As the afternoon wore on, the answer became all too apparent. Early in the half Illinois star Kendall Gill, making only his second appearance since missing most of the Big Ten season with a broken foot, entered the game. From that point on, it was Illinois which did the romping. Placing five players in double figures, the Illini humiliated Michigan, 89–73, the Wolverines' worst

It wasn't Terry Mills' scoring as much as his passing and shot-blocking that helped Michigan beat a pesky Northwestern team.

Big Ten home loss in four years. Rice finished with but 14 points, hitting a very uncharacteristic 6-of-14 field goals. Illinois won the battle of the boards, 37–35, made nine steals, and forced Michigan into 18 turnovers. So complete was the Illini's domination that, after they ran off a string of 14 unanswered points early in the second half, the Crisler crowd began to boo its own team.

The Illini were more gracious. Coach Lou Henson insisted, "Hey, I have always thought Michigan was an outstanding basketball team and I still do. They played good, we just played better." Added Gill, "They're a Final Four team."

But in Michigan's post-game lockerroom, the scene was one of dejection.

"It was an embarrassing loss," said Robinson, who led Michigan with 22 points but scored just eight points in the second half and had only three assists against six turnovers.

"He went back to playing the way he did earlier, and he's got to turn that around," said Frieder. "His assists have got to be twice his turnovers, not the other way around."

Said Robinson: "I don't think I played as well as I'm capable of playing. Things were not going well for me. I was trying to get the rest of the guys into the game, but it seemed like Illinois had momentum the whole game. One thing we have to do better," Robinson added, "is that our team doesn't play defense for nothing. Our defense is lacking tremendously."

Even Rice, who seldom let losses bother him, was obviously down. "It was very emotional for me," he said. "I was real nervous before the game because I didn't know how to handle it. I wanted to smile but I couldn't. It definitely wasn't the way I wanted to go out."

The next day, all eyes would be on CBS' telecast of the NCAA Tournament pairings. Like spring training in baseball, the tournament bracket would speak of renewal to players on most of the 64 teams that would be chosen. For teams that had fallen short of conference championships, teams that had not yet achieved quite what they had hoped to, the second season would begin. The Michigan Wolverines would be among them. Tomorrow there would be hope, even though, as they left Crisler Arena that Saturday evening, their crusade looked like Mission Improbable. Little did they realize that, three days later, it would seem much closer to impossible.

Exit, Bill Frieder

If there was a jokester on the Michigan basketball team, it was Loy Vaught. Vaught's first name, formed by using the first initials of his aunt and uncles, was correctly pronounced to rhyme with Roy. But his teammates called him "Lo" or "Lo-D." Both were abbreviations of his high school nickname, "Lodacious," which was a play on the then-popular "Bodacious." It was easy to see how Vaught had earned such nicknames. Although he had his serious, sensitive side, Vaught also could be, on and off the court, funny, flamboyant, and a little outrageous. Like the time when, as a sophomore, he purposely dismantled a crippled hoop with a ferocious slam dunk in the NCAA Tournament in Charlotte, North Carolina. During the plane trip to the Great Alaska Shootout in his sophomore season, Vaught—who had a prodigious appetite that belied his lean, muscular body—bounced from seat to seat, asking teammates and acquaintances to request second meals. "These little meals they give you on planes just aren't enough," said Vaught, who consumed nine dinners before flight attendants finally cut him off. He could do good impressions of coach Bill Frieder and assistant coach Steve Fisher, and he would crack teammates up by imitating the coaches' pep talks while the team was riding on buses to or from arenas. Sometimes on bus or plane rides, Vaught would make up raps. Sometimes on the road, Vaught would sell teammates on the idea of going to see a movie, only to "discover" at the theater that he'd forgotten his wallet.

So on Tuesday evening March 15, three days after Michigan's loss to Illinois and three days before the Wolverines were to play Xavier in the NCAA Tournament, when Loy Vaught told his teammates that Frieder was leaving Michigan to take the Arizona State job, they didn't exactly take it as the Gospel. As Terry Mills would say later, "I didn't believe it just because Loy was the one saying it. You know, consider the source." There had been rumors that

43

On the court, Loy Vaught was a strong rebounder and a great shooter. Off it, he was Michigan's top jokester.

Co-captain Mark Hughes was one of the Wolverines who got an unexpected wakeup call from their coach.

Frieder was a candidate for the job, but those rumors had seemed to die down a week or two before. And there were always rumors circulating about such things, and most of them turned out to be just rumors. Even when Vaught started offering to bet money on it, the other players were skeptical.

But Vaught was serious. And he was right. He had been tipped off by a reporter at approximately 7 P.M., just a couple of hours after Michigan's afternoon practice—which Frieder had attended—and only two hours before the team was to gather at Crisler Arena to watch films.

"I'll tell you what," Vaught told his teammates, "wait and see if Frieder is here for films. You know he never misses these. If he's not here, you'll know something is up. And that something is that he's in the air right now, flying out to Arizona."

At about 9 P.M., the Wolverines gathered to watch films. Fisher, who usually ran those sessions, got things started. Frieder was not there. After a few minutes, hardly any of the players were paying attention to the film, as whispers buzzed around the room. Glen Rice said fairly loudly, "Where's Frieder?" Fisher either didn't hear him or ignored him. A moment later, another player asked the same question; then another. Fisher said, "Don't worry about that, let's just concentrate on these films."

As the players left Crisler Arena, Vaught was grinning. "Bet it'll be on TV tonight," he said. Other players were shaking their heads. Not too many took him seriously. Most figured Frieder was off attending to tournament details or scouting a possible recruit.

Meanwhile, reporters from Michigan and Arizona were burning up the telephone lines, trading information, hunches and gossip, and coming to the startling realization that Frieder was, indeed, on his way to Tempe, where Arizona State had called a press conference for early the next morning.

At approximately 10:30 P.M., a reporter called Mark Hughes, a co-captain, at his off-campus apartment. Hughes said Frieder hadn't told the team anything about leaving. "I'm sure he'd tell us before he'd do something like that," Hughes said.

Another Wolverine received a call from the same reporter a few minutes later. This player said he suspected that something was up. In the past few weeks, the player said, Frieder hadn't spent as much time at practices and hadn't been as involved when he was there. "He's been on the phone a lot lately, sometimes even at halftime of our games," the player said.

During their 11 P.M. newscasts, Detroit television stations said there were unconfirmed reports that Frieder was headed to Arizona State. At about that same time, Bo Schembechler received an anonymous call telling him the same thing. "I don't think that's accurate," Schembechler told the caller. "He hasn't said anything to me. Why, he's getting his team ready to play in the tournament."

Meanwhile, Michigan players' phones were ringing steadily, as reporters sought them out for comment. Between 1 A.M. and 3 A.M. one caller, who said he worked for *Sports Illustrated*, asked particularly tough questions. He kept manager Greg Taylor on the phone for nearly a half-hour, accusing him of trying to cover up a scandal that was about to break wide open. He seemed to know a great deal about the team, and he asked all sorts of questions about Frieder. If players were reluctant to comment, he badgered them about freedom of the press and the First Amendment, telling them they had a duty to answer his questions.

This caller phoned players, managers, players' girlfriends, even assistant coach Brian Dutcher. One by one, they fielded his questions and then hung up, puzzled. Some of them thought there was something familiar about the reporter's voice. After each call, on the other end of the line, Loy Vaught hung up his phone, laughing. Friends who had been listening in on extensions did the same. Then Vaught's phone rang. The caller identified himself as a reporter for the *Michigan Daily*, the college paper. He asked questions and Vaught answered them for several minutes, until he realized he was talking to Mike Griffin. "I got caught in my own little game," Vaught laughed later.

To put it mildly, it was an unusual night. As Michigan players turned in, they wondered just what the truth was. Were the news reports accurate? Was Frieder really leaving? The players had to be at Crisler Arena the next morning for a practice session. Then they would leave for Atlanta, where they were to play Xavier in a NCAA Tournament first-round game Friday afternoon. They could have used some rest, but they weren't destined to get too much that night. Between 3 A.M. and 5 A.M. many of their phones rang again. This time the voice on the other end had the unmistakable rasp of their head coach.

Hughes was one of those players. He answered his phone at 3:30 A.M., an unusual calling time for most people, but not Frieder.

"Hey, pardner," Frieder said, "are you sleeping?"

"Coach, it's 3:30 in the morning. Of course I was sleeping."

"Well," Frieder said, "I guess you heard about it."

"Yeah, I did," Hughes said. "But it's hard for me to believe."

"Well, it's true. I had to do it, Mark. For my family. I hope you understand. I've got to go to a press conference out here in a few hours. Then I'm coming to Atlanta to coach the team."

"Okay, Coach, that's good. I'll see you."

What neither Hughes nor Frieder knew then was that the next time they saw each other, Frieder would no longer be the Michigan coach.

Bill and Bo

Bill Frieder's odyssey to Arizona State, or somewhere, probably became inevitable on the spring day in 1988 when the University of Michigan announced that its new athletic director would be Glenn E. "Bo" Schembechler.

The winningest active Division I football coach in the country, Schembechler was a living legend in Ann Arbor and, indeed, throughout much of the country. When Schembechler attended Michigan's NCAA Tournament regional final game against Virginia, students greeted him with chants of "Bo is God." From Michigan's perspective, they weren't far wrong. After 20 years of guiding the football Wolverines, he had become a larger than life personage. Not only were his teams overwhelmingly successful, but Schembechler was renowned for his integrity and his outspoken opinions. He was a man's man, an imposing figure who commanded respect. By the late 1980s, he had become a man who was regarded as a spokesman for all that was good about college athletics, not only at Michigan but on a nationwide basis.

Just how powerful was Schembechler?

In the summer of 1987, when the NCAA Presidents' Commission called a special convention—something almost unheard of—to lobby for cutbacks in college sports, Schembechler was invited to the Dallas meeting to speak for football coaches. Among the commission's proposals were cuts in football scholarships and assistant coaches. Like everyone else on the panel, Schembechler was given five minutes to get his message across to a convention that seemed to be leaning toward many of the commission's recommendations. Schembechler spoke for nearly 20 minutes, arguing against the proposed cuts. Afterward Jim Valvano, North Carolina State athletic director and basketball coach, hurried up to Schembechler and pumped his hand. "That was great, Bo," Valvano beamed. "By the time you were done, I was ready to run out there and hit somebody from Ohio State!" Singlehandedly, Schembechler had

When Bill Frieder hosted a retirement/birthday party for Don Canham in the spring of 1988, Frieder, Bo Schembechler, and Canham got together.

The Michigan coaching braintrust: Bill Frieder in the huddle, surrounded by Mike Boyd and Steve Fisher, with J.P. Oosterbaan in the background.

turned the whole convention around. Virtually none of the proposals passed, and the Presidents' Commission emerged looking ill-prepared and ineffectual.

During 1987–88, as Michigan officials searched for a successor to Don Canham, the innovative and hugely successful athletic director who was about to retire, there was a great deal of sentiment for giving the job to Schembechler. But the university's Board of Regents, concerned that no one man could handle both jobs, stipulated that Schembechler would have to relinquish his coaching duties. Politely but firmly, Schembechler declined, saying that although he wanted to serve Michigan any way he could, coaching was his first love. Incensed alumni besieged university officials, demanding that Schembechler be given the job on his own terms. Several months later, a compromise was reached. Schembechler would become athletic director and would be allowed to continue coaching while his friend Jack Weidenbach, a long-time Michigan administrator, would be brought in to oversee the athletic department on a day-to-day basis.

To most fans, there was nothing to indicate that Schembechler's appointment would mean trouble for Frieder. Perhaps Frieder himself didn't see the handwriting on the wall at the time. He had said all along that Schembechler was the right man for the job, and he praised his appointment. But insiders, especially those close to Schembechler, knew that storm warnings had been posted. *Detroit News* sports editor Joe Falls, who had exceptionally good access to Schembechler, wrote a column rehashing Frieder's flirtation with Texas and warning that Schembechler wouldn't put up with such happenings. "When I read that column, I said to someone who knows Bo well that it was silly because Bill and Bo were friends," said Jerry Ashby, a close friend of Frieder's. "And they told me, 'Maybe Bill considers himself Bo's friend. But Bo doesn't see it that way.' That was my first inkling that something might be wrong."

What was wrong, in essence, was that Bill Frieder and Bo Schembechler were like oil and water. When both were merely coaches, they could coexist. When placed in the position where one had to answer to the other, there was no way they were going to mix. "I never had any problem with him," Schembechler said a few weeks after Frieder's departure. "But I think he anticipated he would have problems with me, and that's what prompted all this. And probably, he was right."

The men's differences went right to their respective cores. Schembechler was the quintessential corporate coach, a man who was at home in boardrooms, was involved with charitable organizations, a man to whom image was exceedingly important, a man who demanded that his players wear coats and ties while traveling. Frieder was an energetic and eccentric entrepreneur, a street-smart hustler who was adept at finding and milking every possible angle. As a youngster working at his father's produce business, Frieder knew exactly what to do when, at the close of business, he was left with unsold and deteriorating merchandise: he simply took it into poor neighborhoods, where the lighting was bad, and sold it at discount prices. Not only did Frieder not have a dress code for his players, he often went around looking like an unmade bed. "For years, Bill would wear anything he could get for free," said Frieder's wife, Janice. Said Schembechler: "There were things that Bill Frieder did that I don't believe in. The way he dressed, acted and traveled, the things that interested him. You should be well dressed. Maybe you're more comfortable in a sweatsuit, but it's not in the best interest of the university."

Frieder and Schembechler also differed in their approaches toward their players. Schembechler readily described himself as an old-fashioned coach, and he was known as a disciplinarian. Frieder dealt with players at their own level, often joking around with them and allowing them to say and do things that would never have been permitted by Schembechler. In fact, Frieder may have been too much of a friend to his players. "Maybe that hurt him from the coaching side of it," said assistant coach Mike Boyd. "There are times when a coach has to be a jerk on the floor. Sometimes when you're a jerk on the floor but a friend off it, I don't know how much of what you say on the floor gets through."

Consumed by basketball, Frieder was largely oblivious to the world outside the arena, except for his family and business interests. "If it doesn't help me win games, I don't care about it," was one of his favorite remarks. In Ann Arbor, a city that may have more movie theaters per capita than any other in the nation, Frieder bragged that he hadn't seen a movie since *The Godfather.* That was probably true, partly because the frenetic Frieder could never sit still long enough to watch one. Here was a man who never wore a coat, even during Michigan's sometimes brutal winters, because he felt putting them on and taking them off wasted too much time. Frieder had little patience for social conventions or tact. Virtually nothing offended Frieder, and he was often amazed when something he said bothered other people. When combined with his penchant for trying to be funny, the results could be disastrous. So it was during the week leading up to the first Michigan-Illinois game, when Frieder told reporters he would bet $500 that the Illini would beat his team. When columnists and commentators said such talk was unbecoming a college coach, Frieder was astounded. In the spring of 1988, when word leaked out that Indiana's Jay Edwards had been suspended and sent into drug rehabilitation, Frieder told a reporter, "You can bet he'll be back when we play in Bloomington. If he has a good game, maybe I should say in my press conference 'Hey, I guess that cocaine isn't so bad after all.'" Frieder seemed genuinely puzzled when the reporter advised him against saying that.

Yet Frieder also was an enjoyable guy to be around. He could be charming and witty. Reporters covering the Wolverines quickly found out that one of the best ways to kill time on road trips was to hang around Frieder's room, where the coach would lie on his bed and hold court, regaling listeners with

The Michigan coaching staff: Mike Boyd, Bill Frieder, Steve Fisher, and Brian Dutcher.

funny story after funny story. Frieder was a guy who obviously enjoyed his life very much, a guy who would go to great lengths for a joke. Reporters—especially the *Detroit News'* Jim Spadafore, who had covered him since his days as a high school coach—were frequent Frieder targets. When Michigan played in the Great Alaska Shootout in 1987, Frieder told Spadafore that he hated Anchorage, that it was a dark and dreary place that led to suicidal thoughts, and that he wouldn't come back even if the Final Four were held there. Then he told one of Spadafore's competitors that he loved Alaska and couldn't wait to get back. Spadafore's story was picked up nationally, prompting enraged Alaskans to write complaining letters to Frieder. His response? He sent them copies of the other reporter's story and told them Spadafore had misquoted him. At Michigan's pre-season media day in 1988, Frieder opened his remarks by telling the assembled press corps of his latest recruiting coup, a little-known player with an odd name from some small Ohio town. Only after scurrying around and checking with several sources did reporters discover that no such player existed. Many reporters enjoyed trying to match Frieder's mind games, but others did not. Some suspected—often rightly—that Frieder was trying to manipulate them, and they resented it. But most seemed to enjoy Frieder and his unusual openess—and of course his quotes, whether they were intended or not.

Frieder may have been enjoying himself, and many others may have been enjoying his antics. But some of them were bound to rub someone like Schembechler the wrong way. For Frieder was also something of a loose cannon, a potentially embarrassing firecracker who could go off at any moment.

During the 1986–87 season, when Iowa played at Michigan, Frieder thought he saw Hawkeyes' guard Jeff Moe take a cheap shot at one of his players. Frieder let loose with a stream of obscenities. As luck would have it, national television cameras were focused on him at the moment. Viewers didn't need advanced degrees in lip reading to know that what Frieder was calling Moe wasn't very nice. After a barrage of criticism, Frieder wrote a letter of apology to Moe and Iowa officials. Later that season, the Wolverines were sent to NCAA Tournament competition in Charlotte, North Carolina. When they arrived at their assigned hotel, they found that some of the promised arrangements hadn't been made. Frieder pitched a fit, ranting so long and loud that hotel security was finally called. For the rest of the team's stay, he purposely mispronounced "Charlotte," gleefully noting how the local media and tournament officials cringed whenever he called it "Char-LOT." After North Carolina eliminated the Wolverines, Frieder capped off his post-game press conference by saying, "Well, at least now we can get the hell out of Char-LOT." In the weeks that followed, several Charlotte citizens fired off letters of protest to Canham and Michigan president Harold Shapiro.

Of course, Schembechler himself wasn't always a model of decorum on the sidelines or at his post-game press conferences. He was a man who had been accused of offenses ranging from unsportsmanlike conduct to pushing a student newspaper reporter. But he had mellowed somewhat over the years. And as he said, his perspective changed when he became athletic director. "I had kind of watched (Frieder) from a distance, but I took a more interested role after I became athletic director because everyone told me I was inheriting problems," Schembechler said.

Problems with Frieder were something Schembechler didn't need, especially during the 1988–89 season. Not only was he in his first year as athletic director, but Schembechler was in the midst of trying to raise funds for a new $12 million football building. And lurking in the background, unbeknownst to most people, was the fact that the Big Ten was investigating the Michigan baseball program for alleged recruiting violations. That tied in with another of Schembechler's concerns—the rumors of cheating that seemed to dog Frieder's program. Most likely, those rumors were started by rivals who couldn't accept that Frieder's phenomenal recruiting success had been achieved legitimately. Nevertheless, they kept cropping up. While Don Canham was athletic director, the university had taken some of the rumors seriously enough to launch an internal investigation. It turned up nothing. Shortly after Frieder took the ASU job, rumors were circulating about his wooing of a top Detroit recruit. Schembechler looked into the matter himself during the NCAA Tournament, and decided the university had done nothing wrong. But as the athletic director at Michigan, a university which prided itself on having never been reprimanded by the NCAA, Schembechler would have preferred not to have needed to look into anything. "If somebody came to me and told me (Indiana football coach) Bill Mallory was cheating, I don't give them the time of day," he said. "There are just some guys . . . but in basketball . . . I think all of us would be surprised if Dean Smith or Mike Krzyzewski, Bob Knight or Digger Phelps, guys like that, cheated. I just don't want to hear that kind of stuff about our school."

During the Canham years, Frieder had enjoyed almost unqualified support from his athletic director. That may have been partially because Frieder and Canham were, in some ways, kindred spirits: always-hustling entrepreneurs, straight talking, shoot-from-the-hip guys who were willing to say what they meant and let the chips fall where they may. In Frieder's second year as head coach, the Wolverines struggled to a lowly 7–20 record. At one point, they lost 11 straight games. During that stretch, Canham wrote Frieder a note that said, in essence: "Don't worry what the fans and media are saying. You're my head coach and you're going to remain my head coach. Hang in there and I know things are going to turn around for you." Frieder valued that note so highly that he carried it with him for years afterward. But in his ninth season as head coach, as the criticism mounted despite a much, much better record, there would be no such notes from Schembechler. In fact, as far as many athletic department sources could tell, there was virtually no communication

Bill Frieder and daughter Laura with another famous Michigan alumnus, former President Gerald R. Ford.

Not all of the media knew what to make of Bill Frieder. ESPN analyst Dick Vitale sometimes praised Frieder but regularly chided him for playing a "cupcake" non-conference schedule.

at all between the two men. Then, too, under Canham, as long as the basket-ball program was successful, Frieder was allowed to run it pretty much as he saw fit. But things would be different under Schembechler.

One of the first warning signals came in the spring of 1988, shortly after the Texas fiasco. *Ann Arbor News* writer Jeff Mortimer had been following Frieder and the Wolverines all season so that he could write Frieder's auto-biography, appropriately titled *Basket Case*. The project was nearing comple-tion when Schembechler met with Frieder and tried to talk him out of doing the book. "I didn't tell him not to do it," Schembechler said. "But when that Texas thing came up, he did himself a lot of damage with public support. I just felt that wasn't the right time for him to come out with a book." Never-theless, Frieder and Mortimer proceeded with the book, which was published in the fall.

As basketball season neared, other things were happening behind the scenes. "There were changes made in the program. My personal feeling is, we fre-quently heard about these changes from people in the community before Bill heard about them from Bo," said Janice Frieder. "Bill would be disappointed. Not mad, not angry, but disappointed." Schembechler placed restrictions on game-day visitors in the tunnel outside the Wolverines' Crisler Arena locker-room, and on non-athletic department people riding on team charter planes. He sliced the number of tickets Frieder was allowed to sell or give away. And he was publicly critical of Michigan's pre-Big Ten schedule, saying Frieder should schedule more big-time opponents and fewer weak Division I or Divi-sion II teams. Before the season ended, Schembechler would take scheduling out of Frieder's hands and entrust it to athletic department personnel.

One part of the schedule Schembechler couldn't criticize was Michigan's season-opening appearance in the Maui Classic. There, Michigan played—and defeated—three top-flight opponents: Vanderbilt, Memphis State, and Ok-lahoma. But Schembechler did dispatch an aide, Jeff Long, to accompany the team to Maui. Later, Schembechler would say he sent Long—who also accom-panied the football team on road trips—merely to help with travel arrange-ments. If Frieder thought there was anything else behind it, Schembechler said, "he was being paranoid." At any rate, Frieder responded to Long's pres-ence by tightening the reins on his team. Even after they had beaten Okla-homa to win the Classic, the Wolverines were not allowed to celebrate. As they returned to Ann Arbor, players groused about not being given enough spare time and about Long, whom they dubbed "Bo's detective." Said Glen Rice: "We might as well have lost, for all the fun we had."

Things improved in December, but only slightly. While the Wolverines chewed up opponents such as Grambling, South Dakota State, and Youngs-town State, columnists and commentators ripped Frieder for what ESPN's Dick Vitale had labeled a "cupcake schedule." At month's end, Frieder sus-pended Sean Higgins for three games for "violations of training rules" that turned out to involve drinking and driving. The Wolverines journeyed to Salt Lake City for the Utah Classic, where their perfect 11–0 start was ended with an embarrassing upset loss to Division II Alaska-Anchorage. Michigan rebounded to beat Holy Cross and open Big Ten play with wins over Northwestern and Minnesota. But then came the Wolverines' sudden, surprising swoon that saw them fall to an early 3–3 conference record.

Suddenly, Michigan basketball wasn't much fun, particularly for Bill Frieder. "All the things being said by the fans and the press bothered him," said Jerry Ashby, Frieder's longtime friend. "Bill's much more sensitive than he shows. Put yourself in his shoes. Here you are, your team has lost only three games and is rated in the Top 10 in the country, and the fans are booing you and saying you can't coach. They're holding up signs saying you should be fired, and your young daughter is sitting there, seeing all this. You know you're respected by other college coaches. You've got to wonder, what more can I do? This year, it got to the point where Bill couldn't say anything. This year was not fun for Bill Frieder."

Frieder allowed his pain to show during a few rare moments midway through the Big Ten season. The scene was a Minneapolis hotel where the Wolverines were spending their one day between road games at Iowa and Minnesota. The night before, Michigan had pulled out a much-needed victory over the Hawkeyes in a game that was as exciting as any played in college basketball that season. The Wolverines had stunned the Iowa faithful by roaring out to a huge first-half lead, only to fritter it away under relentless pressure from the Hawkeyes in the second half. Iowa rallied to send the game into overtime, then quickly took command. But the Wolverines also rallied, behind the 3-point shooting of Sean Higgins, to force a second overtime. Again, Iowa took the lead. But again, Michigan fought back. Finally, Michigan claimed a 108–107 win on a Vaught layup with two seconds left. It had been a tremendously satisfying victory. But its luster had been dulled by peripheral happenings. Before the game, Iowa papers had been filled with stories detailing Frieder's falling popularity among Michigan fans. Writers and radio disc jockeys urged Hawkeye fans to make Frieder feel at home by booing him. They did, but Frieder joked, "They didn't boo me nearly as loudly as the people back at Crisler." Meanwhile, vendors in Carver-Hawkeye Arena were selling what they called "Bill Frieder Memorial Programs" to mark what they said would be Frieder's last trip to Iowa City. An usher angered Frieder when he tried to give the coach one of the programs before the game began.

Then after the game, the *Detroit News* reported in one of its editions that Frieder had made an obscene gesture at the Iowa crowd as he and the Wolverines left the court. The report was wrong, and the paper pulled it from later editions. But the damage had been done. Thousands read of the alleged incident the next day. A Detroit radio station picked up on the story and labeled Frieder its "loser of the day." Angie Fisher heard about that as she drove

Bill Frieder could be a fun guy, as he was during Michigan's media day in November 1988, when he showed that he, too, could dunk—on a six-foot basket.

her son Mark, a close friend of Frieder's daughter Laura, to school. Almost simultaneously, the first reports that Frieder was a candidate for the Arizona State vacancy were surfacing.

On that Friday evening in Minneapolis, Frieder stretched out on a hotel room bed, talking to a reporter. It was a wide-ranging, casual conversation. At one point Frieder said, "You know, if I ever do leave, the fans and the media will be the main reason." Referring to the *Detroit News* story, he said, "That's a reflection on my character, and it's wrong. Everybody believes it, and it's not true, and there's nothing I can do about it. Here I go again, Frieder's a bleeping bad guy. It's just so unfair . . . why the Michigan media . . . it's just like today in the Iowa papers, how many people wrote that Tommy Davis should be fired because he lost to Michigan? Nobody. They're supportive of their team. They just don't appreciate anything at our end. I don't mind if you want to criticize me, say that I can't coach or that my team is lousy. That's fine, but then when they've got to make things up on top of it to make you look bad, that's so wrong. It's unfair. I've got a family, I've got alumni, I've got friends, and they're making me out to be something I'm not. And that's just wrong."

Frieder was wiser to the ways of the media than many coaches are. He knew how to cultivate the press and how to clamp down on it. To reporters he liked, he could be a real charmer, a guy who was always ready with a quote, a guy who would return phone calls—although sometimes in the middle of the night—a guy who knew the value of leaking selected scoops to favored reporters. To media members he didn't like, or was temporarily upset with, he could be close-mouthed, surly and confrontational, although he was seldom uncooperative. But there were things about the media he could never understand or accept. There were times when he seethed privately at what he considered—sometimes rightly—to be a double standard in the way the media treated him and the way it treated Schembechler.

Michigan fullback Leroy Hoard, Most Valuable Player of the 1989 Rose Bowl, once compared being in Bo Schembechler's doghouse to being shadowed by one of those huge, inflated cartoon characters that are pulled in many large parades. "It's like a big old Bo balloon following you around all the time," Hoard said.

Perhaps that was how Bill Frieder felt during his last season at Michigan. Publicly, he seldom complained about the media or the fans, although he often said he didn't believe their criticism was warranted. Publicly, he said nothing about his deteriorating relationship with Schembechler. If someone asked, Frieder would say he and Schembechler got along fine, that there were no problems. But those closest to him knew otherwise.

It may have been, as Janice Frieder said, that "I don't think there was any animosity on Bill's part toward Bo. I think Bill thought he would have a better relationship with Bo than it turned out to be. I think Bill misread Bo."

Especially on the night of March 15.

Westward Ho!

It was toward the tail end of the season that Arizona State athletic director Charles Harris contacted the Michigan athletic department for permission to talk to Frieder about the Sun Devils' head coaching vacancy. That contact was to generate another telling disappointment for the Michigan coach. Although Frieder had given Michigan 16 years of his coaching life, although he had become the second-winningest Wolverines coach ever, although he had built the program into a perennial national powerhouse, the request from ASU didn't prompt senior athletic officials to contact Frieder. There was no one telling him he was a valued employee, no one urging him to remain at Michigan. "When the contact had been made and no one said anything to Bill about staying, I think Bill really began to think more seriously about leaving," Janice Frieder said.

Actually, Harris had been informally courting Frieder for months. A former assistant athletic director at Michigan, Harris and Frieder had been friends for years. During Michigan's search for a successor to Canham, Harris had been a candidate for the job—a fact that later led to speculation that Harris may have pursued Frieder partly as a way of getting back at Michigan officials for not hiring him. But, in fact, Frieder had not been Harris' first choice for the job.

Just a few days before Harris offered the job to Frieder, he offered it to Purdue coach Gene Keady. But on Tuesday morning, Keady appeared at a press conference and announced that he had declined the offer, and would remain at Purdue. A few hours later, Harris was on the phone with Frieder.

Later, Frieder would say Harris had given him just 20 minutes to decide whether he wanted the job. Still later, he would back off that statement, saying there had been a 20-minute time frame, but it wasn't an ultimatum. Either way, Harris was putting pressure on Frieder for a quick decision. Harris himself was under pressure. He had guaranteed influential officials and alumni that he would bring a big-name coach to ASU, then had washed out on top choices such as Keady and Oklahoma's Billy Tubbs. The Sun Devils' basketball program, which had been struggling for years, was near rock bottom and the all-important spring signing period for recruits was only one month away. Harris needed a marquee coach, and he needed him quickly.

The Frieders had known for months that this was a decision they might have to make. Secretly, Bill Frieder had flown to Chicago to meet with Harris and discuss the job. Janice Frieder had flown to Phoenix to size up the area. They had laid the groundwork for making the decision. But when Harris finally called that Tuesday, shortly before Michigan began its daily practice, it was still a difficult choice.

"I called Janice," Frieder would remember later, "and I said, 'You know, I think we have a decision to make.' Then we talked for about 15 minutes, discussed the whole thing, and then I picked up the phone and called back, and said I would take it."

That was at approximately 3 P.M. The Frieders didn't have much time to pack, wrap up a few loose ends, and get to the airport for their flight, the last of the day between Detroit and Phoenix. For an hour or so, Frieder bounced back and forth between practice and his Crisler Arena office, where he made some phone calls and squeezed in an interview with a newspaper reporter. At one point, Fisher asked Frieder if he knew about Keady turning down the ASU job. "That ain't all I know about it," Frieder said. A little later, he pulled Fisher aside and broke the news to him.

Meanwhile, Janice Frieder was getting ready for the trip and trying to decide whether to take their daughter, 10-year-old Laura, along. "She came home from horseback riding and the more I started to think about it, the more I thought she should come with us," Janice Frieder said. "She had some concerns about moving, and I thought it might be good for her to go out there. Then she got in the shower and she started crying. She said, 'I don't like making these decisions. I don't know whether to go with you or stay.'" Then to her father, Laura Frieder said, "Dad, don't take that job. Go out there and tell them they have to hire Keady." A few days later, as he sat in an Atlanta hotel room getting ready to watch a Michigan basketball game as a fan for the first time in 17 years, Frieder's voice would crack and his eyes would grow teary as he recalled that moment. "All I could think to say was, 'Well, I'll work on it.'"

In the end, only Bill and Janice Frieder made the trip. Frieder said later that he'd hoped to keep a lid on things until the ASU press conference the next morning, then fly to Atlanta to meet the team—and the rest of the media—and prepare for Xavier. That wasn't quite the way it went. When the Frieders' Northwest flight touched down in Phoenix, television crews had it well staked out. They did, however, have to use their long lenses: while the other passen-

Angie Fisher and Janice Frieder, the first ladies of Michigan's national championship team.

gers headed to the terminal, the Frieders were escorted from the other side of the plane to the runway, where they were met by Harris and then whisked away in a white Mercedes stretch limousine.

Early the next morning, Frieder called Jack Weidenbach and then Bo Schembechler to inform them of his decision. By then, it was hardly news. Weidenbach and Bruce Madej, Michigan sports information director, had turned on their answering machines around midnight because they were tired of telling reporters and other callers that they knew nothing about Frieder's departure. By early Wednesday morning, his defection was a prime topic on radio programs and in morning newspapers. Weidenbach accepted Frieder's explanation until the coach told him he planned to meet his team in Atlanta. "Bill," Weidenbach said, "I'm not sure Bo is going to allow that." Later, Frieder would say that, from the time he accepted Harris' offer Tuesday afternoon until he talked to Weidenbach early Wednesday morning, the possibility of being replaced as Michigan coach had never occurred to him. That shows just how far apart Frieder and Schembechler truly were.

The decision to replace Frieder was "a five-second job," the athletic director said. "If that's the toughest decision I ever have in this job . . . Not that it was a great decision. It was the only choice, and any man sitting in this chair would've made that choice. There are just two things you need to know about Bill Frieder. One, I did not know he was taking that job. He never informed me. He had an obligation to do that, and he didn't do it. Second, I don't think Frieder was at practice. If he was, he wasn't involved. From what I understand, he missed the last practice and all of the film sessions. You and I know that if we're going to a bowl game, we're going to be at practice each day, we're going to be in there intensely looking at film, we're going to be looking for every edge we can. How can you coach a game when you're not even involved? You can't do that. The important thing was that, from a strategic coaching decision, the best coach for us in that tournament was Steve Fisher. I was more interested, not from a public relations standpoint or from Bill Frieder's standpoint, but for what was good for the team. He has a right to do whatever he wants to do, but I think in fairness he ought to keep people posted about what he's doing. His best chance of coaching in that tournament would've been to keep me posted. He could've said, 'Listen Bo, I'm going to talk to these people and I think they might put pressure on me, but I still want to coach in the tournament.' But he didn't do that. He finally called me at 11 the next morning, and told me not to worry, that they had a jet ready to fly him to Atlanta. I told him, 'You're not coaching; Steve Fisher is going to coach the team because he works with it.' He said he could respect my decision, I wished him luck and that was it."

Frieder said he hadn't called Schembechler sooner because he didn't have his telephone number. The coach said he had tried to call Weidenbach during the night, but had only gotten his answering machine. Schembechler's home

Purdue coach Gene Keady was Arizona State's first choice. When he turned the job down, the door opened for Bill Frieder.

number was a closely guarded secret around the Michigan athletic department, but Schembechler said, "If he didn't have it, he knew people who could've given it to him." As for Frieder's involvement at practice, players would later give it mixed reviews. Some thought he hadn't been as intense toward the end of the season, but others said Frieder was just as involved as he had been in previous years.

In the end, all of that mattered little. For Bill Frieder, who had been converted from business student to basketball fanatic while watching Cazzie Russell and the Wolverines in the 1960s, fate had taken some ironic turns. Nine years earlier, Michigan head coach Johnny Orr had left Ann Arbor for the greener pastures—especially in financial terms—of Iowa State. Frieder had been named head coach immediately—but secretly, because Don Canham knew he was circumventing university regulations that required posting job openings. Now, again secretly, after nine years and 191 victories as head coach, after 16 years with the Wolverines, Frieder was leaving. On the surface, money was again a reason; at Arizona State, Frieder would be paid a base salary of $150,000 compared to the $94,000 he earned at Michigan. But the bottom line was a different story. By leaving Michigan for ASU, a program which had four coaches and only two winning seasons in the last eight years, Frieder was walking away from related earnings, like camps and television programs, that figured to be much more lucrative at Michigan, at least in the short run. Some observers agreed with Frieder's mentor, Orr, who said that Arizona State was "a sleeping giant" that could awaken under Frieder. But when all was said and done, basketball insiders figured Frieder would end up earning approximately $500,000 at ASU compared to the $400,000 he had made at Michigan. By another standard, Frieder's contract at ASU was far superior: at Michigan, Frieder had only a one-year "handshake" contract; at Arizona State, he would have the security of a four-year deal.

Perhaps Frieder's departure was inevitable under any circumstances. Schembechler gave that impression when he said, "It's a misconception that I was out to get him, or make his life miserable for him. I think Frieder was different. I think he's an enjoyable guy to have around. The question is, do you want him coaching your team? It's nice to laugh and joke and be a helluva guy. I used to laugh at him, I used to enjoy him. Then I'd start hearing these things and I'd get nervous." Perhaps Frieder finally decided to listen to some of his coaching friends, such as Eddie Sutton and Gene Bartow, who had advised him years before to consider leaving Michigan, telling him how changing scenery could benefit a coach. Perhaps very few basketball coaches are destined to stay long in any one spot, especially if that spot is Michigan. "He will be mourned even less than Orr was, who was mourned even less than Dave Strack, Orr's predecessor (who made it to the Final Four twice in the mid-1960s)," wrote Jeff Mortimer, author of *Pigeons, Bloody Noses and Little Skinny Kids*, a history of Michigan basketball. "There is

Bo Schembechler made it clear: Only a Michigan man would coach his basketball team.

something about a Michigan basketball fan that does not love the coach, no matter who he is."

At any rate, Frieder would not have to concern himself with such things anymore. He was no longer the Michigan coach. Schembechler made that perfectly clear during a Wednesday afternoon press conference, explaining his decision to replace the coach by saying, "I don't want someone from Arizona State coaching my team. A Michigan man will coach the Michigan basketball team." For Frieder, a native Michigander and the holder of two degrees from the U-M, such words had to be hard to take. Later, Frieder would say he sometimes wished he had lied about the ASU job, or had challenged Schembechler's decision to replace him, so that he could've remained with his team through the NCAA Tournament. But he did neither. The die had been cast. Nine years before, Frieder, who had been a Michigan assistant for seven years, was promoted to head coach. On March 16, 1989, another man who had been an assistant for seven years was made Michigan's head coach. His name was Steve Fisher.

"He Became Everyman"

Two months later, Bo Schembechler sat behind his desk, shaking his head good-naturedly. "Wasn't it something," Schembechler said, "the way everybody took to Steve Fisher?"

Indeed it was. An unknown assistant on March 15, Fisher in the next few weeks became a household name, a familiar face, almost an American hero. Here was a man who had never served one single game as a college head coach, suddenly placed in command during the most pressure-packed time of the season, under some of the most pressure-packed circumstances imaginable. Naturally, fans sympathized with him from the beginning. And with each win, he became more and more popular.

"He became Everyman," said Les Wothke, head coach at Army and Fisher's longtime friend and mentor. "He was easy to identify with because probably all of us have thought from time to time, 'I wish my boss would quit. I could do this job better than him.'"

When Schembechler named Fisher interim coach, Wothke was probably the second-happiest coach in America. He knew his friend was being placed in a tough spot, but he also knew what a potentially great spot it was. And he knew Fisher could handle it; in fact, Wothke thought Fisher was ready to be head coach nearly 10 years before.

But Steve Fisher wasn't exactly a fast-tracker. "To tell you the truth," he said, "I could've stayed at Rich East (a suburban Chicago high school) forever. I was there 11 years, eight as head coach. I met my wife there, she taught at the same school. We bought a house three years before we left. We had a good income, there was no pressure, they liked us there. We could easily have kept grinding that rut a little deeper every year, to where it would've been hard to leave. Had Les Wothke not gotten the Western Michigan job, I probably never would have left Rich East because I was happy there. If someone else had been at Western Michigan, I never would have called and applied. Then when I was there, I was happy. I could've ended my career at Western Michigan and never gone any farther. I could've been very pleased that I made that move and had experienced what life was like at that level." Not that Fisher wasn't ambitious. "He always wanted to be a head coach, to be the top guy," Wothke said. But Fisher wasn't driven by his ambition. Bill Frieder, burning to succeed, was unable to jump in a car and drive anything less than 10 or 20 miles per hour over the speed limit. Steve Fisher wanted to succeed, too, but not only could he drive sanely, he taught drivers' education as a high school teacher.

Fisher came by his small-town persona honestly. The second son of three sons and one daughter born to George and Louise Fisher, he grew up in the small southern Illinois town of Herrin, in an area where farming and coal-mining predominated. As a boy, Steve Fisher discovered he was a good basketball player, and during his high school days he nurtured the same dream so many boys do, the dream of going away on a full scholarship to some big-time power such as Missouri or Illinois. But in his senior season, Fisher blew out a knee. He tried to return too quickly, blew it out again, and ended up missing two-thirds of his final year. The dreams of a big-time college scholarship had been killed.

Instead, Fisher went to Illinois State. He played basketball there, but he was never a star. "He was a good player with a bad wheel," said Wothke, who got to know Fisher during those days. "There aren't any memorable nights in his career but he was a solid player, and he was good enough to play major college basketball."

Wothke, then coaching at Bloomington High and managing a country club in the off-season, took a liking to Fisher. He hired Fisher during his graduate student years to tend bar and manage the pool at the country club. It was an incongruous setting for the small-town boy. "He was a terrible bartender," Wothke recalled. "He was personable; that was his biggest plus. He could draw a beer without any problems, but after that he was over his head. As for golf, whenever we would play I would call the groundskeeper and tell him to get extra people out there. I often kidded Steve that *National Geographic* could make films about where we had to go to find some of the balls he lost." And as for managing the pool: "I did it all summer without ever getting in," Fisher would remember. But the future Michigan coach was impressive in other ways. "Before he got married, Steve was one of the most eligible bachelors in suburban Chicago," Wothke said. "I don't want to get into details of his social life, but I will say this: We all marvelled at him."

Meanwhile, the friendship between Wothke and Fisher was growing steadily, especially after Fisher married Angie Wilson, who was a close friend of Wothke's wife. "Angie made Steve Fisher," Wothke said. "She really put a direction into his life. Not that he was without direction before, but she just had such a great influ-

After 10 years as an assistant, Steve Fisher suddenly was a head coach. In the background are Joe Czupek, graduate assistant, and Mike Boyd, assistant.

Steve Fisher was devoted to his family: sons Mark and Jonathan and wife Angie.

ence on him. He has a lot more class now than he did then, and it's because of Angie. She is his biggest fan, his most loyal fan, and also his biggest critic."

After Wothke took over as head coach at Rich East, he hired Fisher as an assistant. Two years later, Wothke took the job as head coach at Winona State. Although Fisher thought he deserved to succeed Wothke, the school instead hired Gene Smithson, who would also go on to become a college head coach. Smithson left Rich East after one season, and this time Fisher got the job. In the next eight years, he became the winningest coach in school history, chalking up a 141–70 record and winning four conference championships. So impressive was Fisher that when he was named Michigan's interim coach over 10 years later, the athletic director of one of his former competitors dashed off a two-page letter to Schembechler detailing why he should make Fisher his permanent choice. He was impressive in other ways, too. At Rich East, he was named tennis coach although he knew practically nothing about the game. He threw himself into the task, learning all he could by first learning about the game from a player's point of view. He became both a good tennis player and a good tennis coach whose teams were quite successful.

When Wothke interviewed for the head coaching job at Western Michigan, he and his wife stayed with the Fishers. A few days later, Wothke called Fisher. He had been given the job, and he wondered if Fisher would like to be one of his assistants. So the Fishers moved to Kalamazoo to rejoin the Wothkes. They were there for three seasons, winning one Mid-American Conference championship along the way. Then Wothke got the Army job. Again, he invited Fisher to be his assistant. But in the meantime, Fisher had gotten to know Bill Frieder, and Frieder had offered him a job at Michigan. The Big Ten beckoned, and Fisher headed for Ann Arbor.

For the next seven years, Steve Fisher labored in relative obscurity. Frieder was the kind of coach who delegated duties, and he valued Fisher highly. So Frieder gave him a wide range of responsibility and authority. Fisher was involved in virtually every aspect of the Michigan program, from recruiting to running summer camps. During games, Fisher would sit next to Frieder, frequently making suggestions and often talking to the team during time-outs. It was important experience, the kind of experience that would prove extremely valuable when Fisher was suddenly called on to guide the team in the NCAA Tournament.

Like everyone else, Wothke had to be surprised by the Fisher fairy tale in the NCAA tourney. But he was not as surprised as many people, because he knew Fisher and he felt that Fisher had all the tools to be a fine head coach. "I think his biggest asset is his consistency," Wothke said. "He doesn't waver. I don't mean he's not flexible. But you know what's expected from Steve, and you always know where you stand. There's no star system in his coaching. He expects everyone on the team to work hard. I think that consistency is excellent in coaching. He also has a very, very basic understanding of the

Although he was only Michigan's interim coach, Steve Fisher made it clear from the beginning that he wanted the job on a long-term basis.

game, and tremendous work habits. He's a student of the game, and he's become a psychologist at it, too. That rapport he developed with the Michigan players wasn't just something that happened in the last six games. He worked for a long time to establish it. For years, he was always trying to develop his own philosophy of the game, and I think he's come up with a mental approach that is very good. He was always a guy whose idea was not to chew somebody out for a mistake, but to correct it. He could get on you and ride you unmercifully. He's a tough sucker. But at the end, he'll pat you on the back or give you a rub on the head."

Off the court, Fisher was a devoted family man who spent most of his free time with his sons, 10-year-old Mark and 3-year-old Jonathan. He would play tennis for hours with Mark, and he treasured the times when he could get away for a walk with Jonathan. But in the first few weeks after Frieder's departure, there wasn't much time for such things. For the next few weeks—during which he lost approximately 15 pounds—basketball would consume Fisher's life as it never had before.

A Family Affair

When Terry Mills pulled into the Crisler Arena parking lot the morning of Wednesday, March 16, he thought there was an unusual number of cars parked there. "All of a sudden, there were reporters all over me," he recalled later. "I don't know if they had been in their cars, all scrunched up so I couldn't see them, or what. But they were all over the place. It was unbelievable." The whole scene was a little unreal as the Wolverines headed to practice that morning. By now, they all knew Frieder had accepted the job at Arizona State. What they didn't know was, who was going to coach them in the NCAA Tournament. Rumors were rampant. "We heard that Coach Frieder was leaving and taking the whole staff with him; we heard that Coach Fisher or Coach Boyd would coach us in the tournament; we even heard that Bo was going to coach us," remembered Mills. Players' reactions varied, but all were surprised, some were hurt and some angry. Rumeal Robinson may have taken Frieder's departure the hardest. All those tutoring sessions had made Janice Frieder "like a mom away from home," he said. Robinson was also closer than many Wolverines to Bill Frieder, even though he hadn't always agreed with his philosophy, and the two of them had clashed at times during the season. "I feel kind of ashamed that as the season went along Coach Frieder took a lot of flak because some of our so-called athletes did not produce to the best of their abilities. We put a lot of pressure on our coach, too," Robinson would say the next day. As the Wolverines gathered in Crisler Arena that Wednesday morning, Robinson fumed, "How do they expect us to do anything in the NCAA Tournament without a head coach?"

He got his answer when Schembechler called the team together at approximately 11 A.M. He explained the situation, told the players that Steve Fisher would be their coach for the rest of the season, told them they were capable of winning the NCAA Tournament, and urged them to put aside the coaching

An example of what assistant coach Mike Boyd called Michigan's "family environment": Mark Fisher and Laura Frieder clown it up under the watchful eye of Sean Higgins.

change and concentrate "on winning the whole damn thing." Schembechler told them: "Remember, you're a Michigan team, and Michigan teams don't go out without a fight."

Ninety minutes later, Schembechler, Fisher, and Mark Hughes appeared before a huge press conference, attended not only by reporters but by practically every employee of the Michigan athletic department. Schembechler outlined the coaching change and said he and Fisher would get together after the NCAA Tournament to evaluate the position on a long-term basis. At that point, Schembechler said he would be committed to getting Michigan "the finest basketball coach in the country." Fisher, who said he had been "totally shocked" by Frieder's defection, said: "We are at a trying time at best. I am now the acting head coach or the coach through the NCAA Tournament. Hopefully, it will be a good, long, strong run. Bill Frieder did a phenomenal job with the basketball program. He leaves tough shoes to step into, for however long or short. But I am hoping it will be long . . . I'm excited and eager. I think it's natural to be nervous, and I am. But I'm also comfortable and confident that our players will work hard, respond, and continue to do what we've been doing." Asked if he hoped to win the job permanently, Fisher said, "Michigan is Michigan, and there's no finer coaching job in the country. I'm not a Michigan grad, but I pride myself now as a Michigan man. Obviously, a long tournament run would help. If we win the national championship, I think that would enhance my chances."

For a team that had just lost its head coach, there was a lot of national championship talk around Ann Arbor that day, although most of it was expressed in facetious tones. Even Fisher's comment was issued with tongue in cheek. Still, Schembechler said, "They're too good a team to go in there and not figure they're going to win this thing." Mark Hughes admitted, "Of course it's going to be a big distraction because it's not every day that a coach leaves a team." But he pledged that the Wolverines were committed to making a strong tournament run. And he said Schembechler's pep talk might help: "That's really the first time I ever listened to Bo. He's very powerful, very emotional. I could tell his talk really hit in with the guys. I think it would be a good idea for him to come in and give us a little pep talk before each game."

Michigan's next game was only 48 hours away. For the players, Frieder, and Fisher—and for all those associated with the program, for all the friends and families—they would be an emotional 48 hours.

Players may have been stunned by Frieder's departure, they may have been angered and frustrated by his timing. But to the surprise of many, they didn't hold the decision against him. "I don't think there's a player in the group who resents him," Fisher said. "They're prepared to deal with it briefly and go on." Said Hughes: "It's very tough for all the players. I feel Coach Frieder had to make the decision that he felt was best for him and his family. He told me he would've liked to have met with us before, but the time frame just wouldn't allow it. He's a great guy and he would've done that had the situation presented itself. I think he had to make the decision quickly, before he wanted to." Later, Loy Vaught said the Wolverines respected Frieder's decision for what he said it was, a business decision: "They say college basketball is big business, and I guess it is," said Vaught. "And the first rule of business is watching out for number one. We kept hearing he and Bo had been having trouble. Arizona State was willing to give him security, to really take care of him and his family. I think he felt that if he didn't take this job, who knew whether he'd be asked back for another year?"

There was another reason the Wolverines didn't hold Frieder's defection against him. Assistant coach Mike Boyd called it the "family environment" Frieder and the coaching staff worked hard to maintain. There was that dimension to the Michigan basketball program. Frieder emphasized unity, togetherness, and in Frieder's scheme of doing things, the players spent a great deal of time together. There were mandatory practices, film sessions, weight-lifting sessions, training table, and study tables. On road trips, it wasn't uncommon for Frieder to call four or five team meetings a day, each 20–30 minutes long, in addition to practices, shootarounds, and study tables. He liked to keep his players together, active and focused; on weekend nights before home games, the team would stay at a downtown Ann Arbor hotel. Knowing that his players would be together so much, Frieder took great care in recruiting players who would fit in. When potential recruits made their campus visits, they were carefully matched up with several players and afterward the players were quizzed on how they felt toward the recruits. There were times when the Wolverines would turn away more talented athletes in favor of players who would fit in better as role players. "I could probably win more games if I'd recruit bleeps," Frieder once said, "but I'm around these guys too much. I don't need to spend my time with a bunch of bleeps."

Janice Frieder and their daughter Laura attended many practices and made most road trips with the team, as did Steve Fisher's wife, Angie, and their son, Mark. Frieder also made sure to schedule the Wolverines for as many attractive tournaments as possible; in Glen Rice's four seasons at Michigan, he traveled to Hawaii twice, as well as to Alaska, Florida, and Europe. Frieder and his assistants were convinced that trips to Europe were especially helpful because they not only allowed the team some extra "spring practice," but they brought the players together for a couple of weeks in the most vacation-like setting they could experience as college basketball players. The Wolverines went on such an excursion in May 1988. "I really think it helped us come together as a team," said Boyd. Later, four-year veteran Mark Hughes would say that this last team was the closest of any he'd played on.

Occasionally, Frieder would end up clashing with a player. But more often, he developed friendships with them. He grew especially close to Gary Grant, so close that he broke down in tears during his pre-game comments before

Mark Hughes was shocked by Frieder's departure, but he was fired up by Bo Schembechler's pep talk.

Grant's last home game. On Frieder's last Michigan team, Glen Rice, Mark Hughes, and Rumeal Robinson were especially close to him. Loy Vaught had a hot-and-cold relationship with Frieder. Vaught often thought he deserved more playing time than Frieder gave him, and "I probably went to him about transferring three or four times," Vaught said. "Every time, he basically told me he wouldn't let me. Then during my junior year, he gave me a starting position and started talking to me more, telling me how next year I was going to be his 40-minute man and all. It really meant a lot to me to have his confidence, after having not had it before. It's funny. We had an up-and-down relationship. We finally started getting along, and he left." Frieder was appreciated, even by players who didn't always see eye-to-eye with him. "One thing about Coach Frieder, if you ever had a problem, you knew you could go to him and talk about it," Vaught said. "And you knew he'd do his best to find a way for you to work it out."

When Terry Mills was a high school star being recruited by virtually every big-time college basketball team in the country, one way Bill Frieder made an impression on him was by writing to him every day for nearly one year. Frieder first met his players when they were in high school and then became one of the dominant figures in their lives as they went through college and climbed toward manhood. He and his players, and his family, spent countless hours together. They enjoyed good times and endured hard times together. They experienced dizzying highs, heartbreaking lows, under incredible pressure together. Frieder cajoled, praised, teased, criticized, and defended them. He advised and taught them. He reprimanded them, he helped them. Inevitably, some strong bonds were formed. Just as inevitably, the Michigan players were riding an emotional rollercoaster as they flew to Atlanta. Not all of the players agreed with Schembechler's decision. Most thought Frieder should have been allowed to continue coaching; some felt they should have been consulted about who should replace Frieder. It wasn't an easy time for the Michigan Wolverines. And it wouldn't get much easier in Atlanta, where they would meet one last time with the man most of them called "Freeds."

Business as Usual

Bill Frieder met his Wolverines at the Atlanta airport. A short while later, they all gathered in a room at the team's hotel: Bill, Janice, and Laura Frieder; players, coaches, managers, coaches' wives, and families. People sat, stood, and sprawled all around the room. As a group, Frieder told everyone what he had told many of them individually: that the Arizona State job, in an area of the country he and Janice had long been fascinated with, had simply been too good an opportunity to pass up; that he wished the timing could have been different; that it had been Schembechler's decision, not his, that he wouldn't coach the team in Atlanta; that he loved them, would miss them, and wished them the best of luck. Laura Frieder broke down in tears, and she wasn't the only one to cry. Later that night Frieder told a press conference: "That was tough . . . I cried and I couldn't get through it. It was tough. But I think they understand and support me, and that means a lot to me because they're the people who know me best." Frieder also told the press he had no ill will for Michigan fans or athletic officials. He said he had tried to be honest about taking the Arizona State job in order to avoid the criticism that had dogged him regarding the Texas job. He also made an ironically prophetic statement when commenting on the pressures of high expectations at Michigan: "I think it's going to take a national championship at Michigan before they accept the next guy."

Frieder promised his players he would be in the stands when they took the floor against Xavier Friday afternoon. "I told the kids I was going to stay all week, but I don't know if I can do that emotionally," Frieder said. "I'm going to that game, but that's going to be a tough thing for me Friday, to be at that game."

It wasn't going to be easy for Steve Fisher, either.

Fisher, who had so firmly set his sights on becoming a college head coach just a few months before, suddenly had his wish—under far different circumstances than he could have ever imagined. He was, he would admit later, "scared to death." But he had a few things going for him. For one thing, Fisher was well prepared to take over. Frieder had given him plenty of responsibility, from running practices to suggesting strategies and lineup changes during games. As part of his responsibilities, he spent hours poring over tape of both Michigan and Wolverines' opponents. Fisher recommended game plans and "broke down" tapes into segments to help each Michigan player with his matchup.

Fisher also knew the players. Although assistant coach Mike Boyd was more heavily involved in recruiting, Fisher had certainly played a part in building Michigan's team. Also, the players knew him. At the time, many of them viewed him as something of a disciplinarian. In Frieder's system, that was the role Fisher had come to play. In many programs, the head coach played the hard-nosed role while assistants were the ones who soothed players' bruised feelings. Michigan's was somewhat the opposite. Although Frieder and his staff didn't define their roles in strict "Good Cop, Bad Cop" terms, Frieder's tendency to be his players' friend naturally led Fisher to balance him by playing the hard guy.

Players also knew Fisher as a guy who could be . . . well . . . boring. "He can go over those films, and over and over them, forever," said Mark Hughes. "He'd see something and he'd run it back and go over it, again and again. Guys would be looking around, guys would be yawning, guys would be sleeping. I'd get Frieder's attention and he'd say something like, 'Okay Steve, I think we can go on to something else now.'" Players also knew Fisher could sometimes fall victim to tunnel vision, as he proved later that week when, deep in concentration, he briefly got lost in The Omni. But by and large, players liked and respected Fisher; they regarded him as a straight-shooter, a guy they could trust.

Fisher had something else going for him: a pretty good basketball team. "Sure they'll miss Bill Frieder," said Xavier coach Pete Gillen, an up-and-coming, funny young coach who ironically was one of the first names bandied about as a possible successor to Frieder. "But a nuclear power is still a nuclear power, no matter who the president is."

The Wolverines didn't play like a nuclear power against Xavier. But they eventually proved to be too powerful for the Musketeers. With Glen Rice and Rumeal Robinson leading the way with 23 points each, the Wolverines slogged their way through a sluggish first half and then caught fire enough to nip Xavier, 92–87. "They can bring in Mark Hughes and (Demetrius) Calip and Sean Higgins," said Gillen. "Cripe, Sean Higgins was a high school All-American. If he was with us we would have erected a statue to him . . . We were tired at the end. The game was like a water torture, and we cracked first. They pounded and we pounded, but they could pound a little longer. Weariness destroys judgment, and we made some bad decisions when we got worn down. We had 19 turnovers, and you're not going to beat a team like Michigan with 19 turnovers."

But for the first two-thirds of the game, it had seemed like that was exactly what the 14th-seeded Musketeers were going to do against the third-seeded Wolverines. With Bo Schembechler watching from a courtside seat and Frieder watching the first half from far up in the stands, Xavier moved to a six-point lead with 9:45 remaining in the game.

Then Calip stepped forward. The little sophomore, an excitable waterbug who tried to make his energy more effective by reading self-help books and listening to motivational tapes, had been in the game twice before, after Robinson got into quick foul trouble. But positive thinking didn't help Calip much on his first two appearances in this game. He had trouble handling the ball against Xavier's quick, pressing guards, and Fisher was forced to substitute for him quickly both times. But when Robinson picked up his fourth foul with 12:36 left in the game, Fisher had little choice. Telling Calip, "Give us the play you used to give Flint Northern," Fisher sent him back in.

This time, Calip came through. With Michigan trailing, 71–65, with 9:35 remaining in the game, Calip drove the baseline for a layup, drew a foul, and turned it into a 3-point play. "That was a big play," said Gillen. "It didn't cost us the game, but it was a big play." So was the offensive rebound the 6–1 Calip grabbed and put in to pull Michigan within 74–73 with 6:08 left. So was the short jumper he swished to give Michigan an 86–83 lead with three minutes left. And so was the pair of free throws he calmly knocked down to make it a 90–85 game with 28 seconds remaining. In 14 total minutes, Calip scored nine points—five in the last three minutes of the game—grabbed two rebounds and notched one assist. "Calip not only played well alongside Rumeal, he did an excellent job when he was in for Rumeal," Fisher said. "It was a critical job, an excellent one for a guy who really hasn't played that much. He has not had that kind of pressure placed on him too many times, and he responded admirably."

So did Terry Mills, who had 18 points, six rebounds, and five assists. His 12 first-half points on a variety of inside moves were almost all that kept Michigan in the game early. "Last night Coach Fisher called me into his room and said he was going to tell the guys to get the ball inside to me, and I should be ready for it," Mills said. "I have to love that, and today I made good decisions when I got it. I felt like somebody had to step forward. They wanted to know if we had enough discipline, character, and class to come out here and win this ball game under the circumstances, and we did."

The circumstances had been unusual, all right. Although he was in the midst of spring football practice, Schembechler jetted to Atlanta on the private plane of Ann Arbor pizza mogul Tom Monaghan, founder of Domino's

Mark Hughes and the Wolverines eventually wore down the Musketeers.

Pizza and a close friend. Through a ticketing quirk, Schembechler and his wife, Millie, were originally given seats directly in front of, and one row removed from, Frieder and his family. Instead, Frieder headed up, eventually standing in the aisle while he nervously watched; Schembechler headed down, finding a seat along press row, where he pounded the back, shoulders, and arms of unsuspecting *Detroit Free Press* columnist Mitch Albom during every important play. "I never realized how strong, physically strong, Schembechler was until he kept slugging me today," Albom moaned. Meanwhile, Michigan's famous fight song "The Victors" was being played by some moonlighting bandsmen from nearby Georgia State. Michigan athletic officials decided to save $15,000 on sending its band and cheerleaders to Atlanta, instead hiring some Georgia State musicians and attiring them in Michigan T-shirts and caps. "I've gotten more letters complaining about that decision than I have about the basketball coach's job," Schembechler groaned.

Meanwhile, Fisher was staking his first, tenuous claim to the job. He walked away from his first game as a college head coach with a win and some high marks. He had weathered having three of his top players—Mills, Robinson, and Loy Vaught—fight foul trouble all day. He had made do even though Vaught, his most accurate shooter, had contributed only 2-of-4 field goals. He had to constantly shuffle his lineup in search of the right combinations against an underrated Xavier team, one that had just the sort of quickness that had given the Wolverines problems all season. "Steve Fisher did a terrific job," said Gillen. "He was in a situation where he had nothing to do but lose, and you've got to give him a lot of credit."

After the game, the Wolverines did just that. As they spoke, the first strands of what would come to be a pattern began to emerge: Fisher was a different coach than Frieder; he was calmer, more positive, and the players liked that. "One thing I noticed about Coach Fisher was that he was a little more relaxed," said Sean Higgins. "And he gave us a little more freedom, which I like. If you made a mistake he'd tell you what you did wrong and say, 'That's okay, do it right next time.' Coach Frieder would have just taken you out."

Said Calip, "A lot had to do with the encouragement I got from Coach Fisher. He didn't get down on me. He just said, 'Hey, don't be afraid to make mistakes. Just play hard.'" That kind of talk meant a great deal to Calip, a very religious young man who, at mid-season, had come very, very close to transferring to neighboring Eastern Michigan.

The previous summer, Calip had worked hard at improving his game. Playing in Ann Arbor's Sandy Sanders Summer Basketball League, he had averaged 30 points and had almost challenged Rice for MVP honors. But Frieder was never really sold on Calip. Once the season started, Frieder gave Calip only a few minutes of mop-up time. And when the Big Ten season began, Calip saw even less action. Meanwhile, Frieder was constantly bemoaning his guard situation, saying that Robinson was the only legitimate guard on the team.

Glen Rice helped Steve Fisher post a win in his first game as a head coach.

"That hurt," Calip admitted later. "Finally, I approached him with the question. I asked him if he thought I was going to play here, and he said no. I was almost gone. And then I talked to some people, and I decided to stay. Academics was one of the reasons I picked Michigan. But basketball is very important to me, too. I read, looked into the Bible, and prayed a lot. I've always felt that if you keep God in your mind, things will work out. Then we ended up winning the national championship, and I was a vital part of it. It must have been meant for me to be here. And Thank God for Coach Fisher. He stuck with me, and I was able to get my game together down the stretch."

Fisher seemed to have his game together the whole way. "Business as usual" had been his theme in preparing for the game, and all in all, he had taken care of business. "I was nervous," he said, "but I didn't sense any added pressure." Well, maybe a little . . ."It seems like the days and nights have run together like a blur," he admitted. "Usually, you know, I'm a real easy sleeper. The last few days, though, I've been tossing and turning all night, waking up at 5:30 or 6 every morning. And it seems I've been eating a lot less. I'm not real big but I can usually eat a lot of food. Lately, I just haven't felt up to eating. I've got a lot of nervous energy, I guess." But once the game started, Fisher said, "I was able to settle into the role very easily. You know, it's not as if I've never coached this game before. I'm 43 years old and I've been coaching for 21 years—eight as a head coach. I'd like to think in all that time I learned a little about coaching." Including a knack for late-game ice-breakers and prophecies that would come in handy a little further along the tournament trail. When a dejected Mills headed to the bench with his fourth foul, Michigan trailed by four with 10 minutes left in the game. "I wanted to pick him up a little bit," Fisher said, "so I leaned over to him and said, 'Hang in there. We're going to win this game by seven points. You watch.'" If the referee hadn't waved off Mark Hughes' last-second basket, the final score would have been Michigan 94, Xavier 87. Fisher had missed his prediction, but he had come close enough. In Michigan's post-game lockerroom, there were many more smiles than there had been in a few days. "Hey, it's always fun when you win," Fisher said. "And I'm 1–0, the best darn winning percentage in the country."

Taming the Jaguars

It was early May before Steve Fisher finally found the time to go back and look at the tapes of the Wolverines' first two NCAA Tournament games. After he did, he quickly put them back in their boxes. "When you look at those games, you realize how very close we came to losing both of them," Fisher said. "It scared me to death."

Fisher was right. The Omni was no place for the faint of heart that weekend. What was needed was a strong stomach, especially for Sunday afternoon's tussle between Michigan and South Alabama.

That may have been the first food fight ever staged for the NCAA tourney. On the one side were South Alabama's cat-quick, high-jumping, high-scoring guards, Junie "Peanut Butter" Lewis and Jeff "Jelly" Hodge. On the other side was the meat-and-potatoes attack of Glen Rice and the Michigan Wolverines. South Alabama was, like Xavier, a team with enough quickness to somewhat negate Michigan's size advantage. Hodge was a slick shooter who had drilled a buzzer-beating 3-pointer to upset Alabama Friday. Lewis was a sneaky-quick leaper, a 6–3 guard with all the moves, who played at about 6–8. The rest of the Jaguars, especially burly 6–7 center Gabriel Estaba of Venezuela, were at least adequate. Coach Ronnie Arrow hadn't compiled the nation's best junior college percentage at San Jacinto Community College by accident. He had the Jaguars come out trying to capitalize quickly on their strengths. Like Indiana had in its second win over Michigan, USA would attack the Michigan defense—especially Robinson. Throughout his first two seasons, Robinson had a tendency to commit needless fouls, most of them when he was whistled for charges. The Jaguars hoped to drive against him on offense, and force him to drive on defense, a strategy that worked.

When Robinson sat down with his second charging foul midway through the first half, Michigan was in the process of letting an early 11-point lead slip away. Not only did the foul sideline Robinson, it put South Alabama in the bonus. Lewis made one of the ensuing free throws to pull USA within 24–22. The Jaguars were charging back into the game. The Wolverines were just charging—or at least that's how officials saw it. Right after Robinson exited with charge number two, Glen Rice was called for the same thing, sending Terrance Brodnick to the line to tie the score. Michigan came roaring back on a fast break that ended in a play the Wolverines would talk about for the rest of the season: 6–1 Demetrius Calip took the ball in on 6–7 Estaba and exploded to the hoop as if powered by Dale Carnegie basketball shoes. Calip went up and up, then came thundering down with a jam that was simply too powerful to be coming from his slight frame. Unfortunately, on the way down he leveled the veteran Estaba, who was well planted—although probably not expecting to pay such a heavy price. But it was Michigan that really paid. Calip's basket was waved off. Michigan was called for its third straight charge, and a few seconds later Estaba hit a turnaround to stake South Alabama to a 26–24 lead.

Only 90 seconds after leaving the lineup, Robinson went back in. Three minutes later, he drew his third foul—for charging—and sat back down. "I went straight up and straight down, and a guy slipped underneath me," Robinson groused later. "What can I do? I have to come down somewhere." Neither he nor any of the Michigan onlookers were too happy. The Wolverines were en route to being called for 17 first-half fouls, compared to five for South Alabama. Sports columnist Mitch Albom should've been glad he wasn't sitting with Schembechler, who had decided to fly to Sunday's game with several of his assistant coaches. They sat around him, and sometimes joined their boss in bolting out of their seats, furious over calls against the Wolverines. After one call, one Michigan assistant leaped out of his aisle seat and ran several steps toward the floor before reining himself in.

At the half, South Alabama led, 47–44. Three Michigan starters—Robinson, Mike Griffin, and Mark Hughes—had three fouls each. Philip Darden had the most fouls of any USA player—two. On the plus side, Michigan was shooting well—60.6 percent—and Rice had gotten off well, hitting 8-of-13 shots for 17 first-half points. On the minus side, USA had outscored much-bigger Michigan, 7–2, in second-chance points, with an 8–4 edge in offensive rebounds. Nobody had been able to stick to "Peanut Butter" Lewis, who had burned the Wolverines for 16 points.

Fisher wasted little time getting across his halftime message: "You guys are doing too much bitching and whining. You worry about playing basketball and let me take care of the other stuff." Later, Fisher would say: "Whether they were good or bad, the calls certainly went against us in the first half. We told them at halftime there was nothing we could do about that. We allowed that to get to us a little in the first half. But you've got to be able to fight that frustration. We couldn't let it take us out of what we were trying

As Michigan took another step along the NCAA Tournament trail, players gave Steve Fisher a good deal of credit for his positive reinforcement.

to do. We just had to keep working hard. We got a couple of calls in the second half."

More than a couple, really. Things evened up considerably in the second half, as USA was hit with 12 fouls and Michigan five. But that wasn't what turned the game around. What turned the Wolverines around was Terry Mills' best game yet and a nice big serving of steaming Rice.

After falling behind by six early in the second half, Michigan finally tied the score at 67–67 with 12:20 left on a baseline jumper by Mills. Four lead changes later, Mills hit a short turnaround and then added a free throw to put Michigan up, 83–80, with 2:17 remaining. Just 12 seconds later, Rice swished a 3-pointer from the top of the circle and Michigan had an 86–80 lead. The Wolverines claimed a 91–82 win, and were on their way back to the Sweet 16. Rice finished with 36 points on 16-of-25 field goals, the most field goals ever scored by a Wolverine in a NCAA Tournament game. He also pulled down eight rebounds, had five assists, and stepped forward at the end of the game to clamp down on Lewis, who ended with 25 points and nine rebounds. Mills, who played the entire second half without drawing another foul, poured in 24 points, grabbed seven rebounds, and handed off five assists. Robinson suffered through his worst game of the tourney with 12 points and five assists, but Calip again helped ease the pain. In 19 minutes, he scored three points, had five assists and only one turnover.

As for coaching: "Don't let anybody tell you Steve doesn't know what he's doing," USA coach Arrow said. "He did a helluva job." Especially down the stretch. With the game on the line, Michigan players liked the way Fisher conducted himself. "He's shown us guidance we haven't had in a while," Robinson said. "He's done a lot for us in terms of coaching and by being a great person. He is calm and he has a lot of confidence in us. We can see it when we come to the sidelines during a timeout. Before, during a close game, the coach would look like he was expecting to lose. We don't see that look now. We feel confident we can pull it off. Coach Fisher believes in us and we believe in him."

Mills certainly had become a Fisher booster, after putting together the best back-to-back performances of his career. "We all love Coach Fisher and we're all playing hard for him," said Mills. That was partly because of a seemingly innocuous change Fisher made for the South Alabama game. For some reason, Frieder had always insisted on listing Mills as a forward, although he was really the team's center. For the USA game, Fisher changed that, listing Mills as center for the first time in his career. "I guess this means Coach Fisher isn't going to play mind games with me," said Mills. "Hey, I'm 6-10 and I'm the biggest guy on the team. I should be the center."

After the game, Fisher said he was pleased by the way his team had scrapped and clawed to come from behind for the win. But he also knew the Wolverines had some problems that had to be solved if their tournament mission

Demetrius Calip drew a charging foul for this slam dunk, but it provided his teammates with one of their most cherished memories of the season.

was going to continue. "It's evident that we need Rumeal out on the floor to be Michigan at its best," Fisher said. "When we got in foul trouble it took us out of the rhythm and continuity we need to be effective. We're going to focus on making sure that, as he dribble-drives and penetrates, he knows when people are attempting to take the charge, and maybe pull up instead of going ahead and forcing and fighting."

Fisher also needed to find a way to get Vaught back into the splendid form he had shown all season. Against USA, Fisher started Hughes ahead of Vaught. Neither fared particularly well, although Vaught did grab seven rebounds. But his sweet shooting touch had abandoned him altogether. He had entered the game with a 69.1 percent field goal percentage, but against USA he hit only 1-of-5 shots.

For 31 minutes, South Alabama had given the Wolverines all they wanted. But in the end, Michigan's size, strength, and depth were just too much. Especially when combined with Rice. "That Rice kid is unbelievable," said Arrow. "We knew he could shoot the ball, but he's going to make somebody a better NBA coach. We were going to try and keep the ball out of his hands, but that's tough when you have to run into a couple of 250-pounders. They have some real men setting picks for him. I thought it was the Atlanta Hawks out there for a while today." Lewis felt the same way. "I covered him half the game when we were in man-to-man," Lewis said. "They picked for him a lot, and it was like running into a brick wall. I tried to belly up on Mills but moved over to pick, and it started to hurt. Rice can flat-out play."

That was something Rice's teammates all knew. When they needed nutrition, they knew where to look for it. "Glen Rice is like the meat of our team," Hughes said, "and the rest of us are the potatoes, gravy, and all the rest of that stuff. That's the point of our team. Glen is the meat, and we keep going back to him. Glen is such a great player, you know if he's open he'll get you some points. We look for number 41 at crunch time, and it's a feeling of relief knowing he's hitting." Rice reacted in his typically modest fashion. "We're all the meat on this team," he said. "No one individual can win the game. My teammates did a great job of looking for me and setting screens for me." As for pressure, Rice said, "I never get nervous. I feel if I ever get nervous, then I'm not the man to go to. But I like it. It's a lot of pressure, but I feel if you can step up to that pressure then you're doing a great job." That was exactly what Rice's teammates expected of him. "He knows he's the go-to man down the stretch," Robinson said. "Glen is something we can count on."

And he was just getting warmed up.

Cooking with Rice

In November 1985, during a season-opening game between Michigan and Virginia Tech in a steamy little gym on the Hawaiian island of Maui, a lithe freshman named Glen Rice took his first official shot as a Michigan Wolverine. It was an airball.

In the next four years, that was a sight that was seldom repeated.

Glen Rice may not have been the greatest player in Michigan history. As practically any Michigan fan will tell you almost reflexively, that honor probably belongs to Cazzie Russell, who was a consensus three-time All-America in the mid-1960s. But by the time Rice's senior season was drawing to a close, he had established himself as one of the best Wolverines ever. What he was destined to accomplish in the NCAA Tournament would propel him to dizzying heights that no one had ever expected him to scale.

No one. Not even Glen Rice. In fact, probably Rice least of all.

On the basketball court, the 6–7, 215-pound Rice was a player apart. A brilliant shooter from anywhere on the floor, he could also rebound and score from inside. On fast breaks, Rice ate up the floor—as well as opponents—with his long strides, acrobatic leaping ability, and explosive dunks.

Rice had his flaws. He was usually adequate on defense but there were times when he was less than adequate, and fewer times when he was good. Some opponents with decent quickness found that driving around Rice wasn't the hardest task in the Big Ten. He had improved his ballhandling, but still wasn't exceptional at it. Perhaps his greatest shortcoming was that, after four years, Rice still hadn't developed a strong move to the hoop.

But Rice played hard, be it practice or game. And he was very coachable. In Rice's sophomore year, new recruit Terry Mills had turned up ineligible due to Proposition 48. Frieder decided to rely on a three-guard offense. Coaches told Rice they would need big rebounding help from him. Although Rice,

Glen Rice may have been quiet off the court, but he was seldom quiet on it.

Even as a sophomore going up against Navy's David Robinson, Glen Rice knew
how to score.

then even slimmer than he was as a senior, readily admitted that he wasn't overly fond of physical contact, he averaged more rebounds that year than any Big Ten player except Illinois' Ken Norman.

And Glen Rice could shoot. Oh, could he shoot. With his height, jumping ability, and range, Rice truly was a bomber, a long-distance destroyer who could stretch opposing defenses and still fire away over them. When Glen Rice was on—as he usually was, with a career field goal percentage of 56.9— he was the kind of player who boosted his teammates to better performances simply because his scoring put so much pressure on other teams' defenses.

"When Glen Rice is on, my first priority is to get him the ball," Gary Grant, Michigan's all-time assists leader, said toward the end of Rice's junior season. "And when Glen Rice is not on, my first priority is still to get him the ball."

Rice certainly knew what to do with it. If anything, Glen Rice on the basketball court was the picture of confidence. He carried himself with pride and grace, and played the same way. During the NCAA Tournament, millions of fans would marvel at how unflinchingly Rice would sink baskets just when Michigan needed them most. But Rice had done that throughout his senior season. And not just the obviously crucial baskets toward the end of games. Whether it was early in the game or late, whether the Wolverines needed the hoop to get back into the game or to stop their opponents' surge, Rice was there to hit it—often with one of his silky smooth, rainbow 3-pointers.

"That's real neat," Rice said of such shots. "I like quieting the other team's crowd down."

As Michigan headed into its third-round NCAA game against North Carolina, Glen Rice had considerable crowd-quieting experience. He also had plenty of NCAA Tournament experience; this would be Rice's 10th NCAA game. Not that Rice had anything against vocal crowds. He enjoyed playing to the fans as much as anybody. Just before the North Carolina game, when he and his teammates took seats behind one Rupp Arena basket during the Oklahoma-Virginia game, approximately 1,000 Michigan fans greeted their appearance with chants of "Let's Go Blue!" Rice responded by giving fans the thumbs-up, and the crowd loved it.

But of all the Wolverines, Rice would've been content to play basketball before any kind of crowd—or before no crowd at all. His love of the game was that great. So great that, a few days after the official opening of practice on October 15, at a time when most players were struggling to adjust to the rigors of the season and were glad for any breaks they could get, Rice was calling to see if any of them wanted to play some pickup ball.

"When he's out there on the court, he's a different person," said Jerry Ashby, a close friend of Frieder's, who frequently drove the coach to scout Rice in high school, then followed the forward's progress from close range at Michigan. "He's flamboyant, aggressive, cocky, all the things he isn't off the floor."

Ironically, the player who would finish his career as the highest scorer in

Glen Rice ended his career as the highest scorer in the history of the Big Ten. Not bad for a guy who wasn't even Michigan's top recruiting target as a high school senior.

Michigan history wasn't a high recruiting priority for the Wolverines until midway through his senior season. That was after Michigan had washed out on Melvin McCants, who picked Purdue, Lowell Hamilton (Illinois), and Roy Marble (Iowa). In his first two seasons on the Flint Northwestern varsity, Rice was overshadowed by older teammates like Jeff Grayer, who went on to become a U.S. Olympian and first-round NBA draft pick, and Andre Rison, who became a star receiver for Michigan State and a first-round NFL draft choice. But as a senior, Rice burst forth in his own right and eventually was named the state's "Mr. Basketball."

Ashby remembered watching Rice then. "During Glen's junior year, the rap on him was that he wasn't a good kid," Ashby said. "Well, we kept seeing him play. And he was never involved in any problems. He never gave anybody any lip. All he did was play basketball. After a while we decided, 'This kid is a great kid.' Glen may have been the only great player to come to Michigan out of high school who didn't think he was a great player. He didn't think he was 10 feet tall. In fact, I remember when he made his visit, he was sitting there watching the guys and he said, 'Boy they're big. I don't know if I can play with them.'"

That wasn't the first time Rice had felt that way. Flint Northwestern coach Grover Kirkland remembered Rice as a 6-4 sophomore: "He was still a little clumsy, and he was still growing. He wanted to stay back on the junior varsity. He walked into that gym and saw all those kids—we usually have hundreds of kids trying out each year—he didn't think he was ready. I had to more or less coax him into the gym."

Rice came by his humility honestly. He was 10 when his mother moved him, his two brothers, and his sister from Arkansas to Flint, one of many Midwestern cities which had been economically devastated during the '70s and '80s. Later, Rice would remember discovering the realities of drugs and weapons at his Flint elementary school. "It was a pretty scary place at first," he said. Rice sought refuge in his family, religion, and basketball. Years later, when he was starring at Michigan, Rice would dedicate much of his time to youth through his church. Meanwhile, his mother Ernestine and his pastor would be in the stands for all of Rice's home games.

"It was tough for us," Rice once said of his Flint childhood. "We really didn't have the things we wanted that other people had. We wanted to have a basketball goal, but we couldn't have a real one so we had to make it out of a coat hanger. Our ball was rolled-up socks. There was one point where I was trying to play basketball and was wearing Trax while everyone else was wearing Pro-Keds or Converse. I had to take a lot of criticism from people joking around with me. I had to work real hard to get to where that didn't bother me."

Rice also had to work hard at the transition from Flint to Ann Arbor, from high school to the University of Michigan.

On the court, things couldn't have gone much more smoothly than they

went for Rice as a freshman. The Wolverines, en route to winning a second straight Big Ten championship, returned a frontline nucleus of Roy Tarpley, Richard Rellford, Butch Wade, and Robert Henderson. In the backcourt, Michigan had Gary Grant, Antoine Joubert, and Garde Thompson. Rice wouldn't be under any pressure to perform immediately. Nevertheless, he played well. Well enough that some observers thought Frieder should have started him ahead of Wade by season's end. Well enough to lead Michigan in scoring in its NCAA win over Akron.

But off the court, things were different. Involved in a fight at a campus recreation building, Rice was charged with assault and sentenced to perform community service. He got into another, less serious, altercation the next summer and struggled to stay academically eligible.

"People were saying we should get rid of Glen Rice," Ashby recalled. "What people didn't understand was that Glen wasn't a bad kid, he was just a street kid. They didn't understand that where Glen comes from, you don't walk away from fights. But Bill, having been a street kid himself, understood."

Frieder stuck with Rice, and it paid off. As a junior, Rice led the Big Ten in scoring. He did it again as a senior, becoming the first Big Ten player to top the conference in scoring in back-to-back seasons since Jay Vincent did it for Michigan State in 1980–81.

By the time he was a senior, Rice epitomized the quiet superstar. On the court or around friends, he could be as loud as any young man. He was much more outgoing generally than he had been early in his college days, but he was still too self-conscious to be what most reporters considered "a good interview." Rice didn't much care to grant interviews anyway. "If you know Glen, he can be real talkative and real funny," said manager Joel Portnoy, a veteran of three seasons with the Wolverines. "Or if you'd ask him about the other players, he'd go on and on. But he doesn't like to talk about himself." Rice's off-court lifestyle didn't provide reporters with much flash, either; his favorite non-basketball interests included playing video games, repairing bikes, watching Chuck Norris movies, and attending church.

Rice hadn't begun to receive national media attention until midway through his junior year, when it seemed for a while that he might become the first Big Ten player in years to lead the conference in both scoring and rebounding. Even during his senior season, he remained relatively unknown to fans outside the Big Ten.

All of that began to change on that Thursday night in Lexington, Kentucky.

If there was a rite of passage for the Michigan Wolverines during the 1989 NCAA Tournament, it was the North Carolina game. In each of the last two seasons, the Tar Heels had knocked the Wolverines out of the tourney. North Carolina was a perennial powerhouse that expected to advance; Michigan was a comparative new kid on the block, still trying to shed its underachieving image. Naturally, the Tar Heels were favored.

Glen Rice started what was to be a sensational senior season by being named the MVP of the Maui Classic.

The task facing interim coach Steve Fisher was a daunting one. In his third game as head coach, he was going up against legendary Dean Smith, who would be coaching his 857th. A few years before, in what was rapidly seeming like another life, Fisher had snuck into a coaches' clinic to get Smith's autograph. "I told him it was for my son, but it was just as much for me," Fisher recalled.

Many observers expected the game to be settled inside the paint. In their previous two meetings, the Wolverines had not had much luck containing North Carolina's powerful J.R. Reid and Scott Williams. The Tar Heels had fared much better against Terry Mills, Loy Vaught, and Mark Hughes.

But it quickly became apparent that this game was going to follow a different script. North Carolina senior guard Jeff Lebo set the tone by banging in five 3-pointers in the first seven minutes. His back-to-back triples staked the Tar Heels to a 26–18 lead with 12:48 remaining.

The record for 3-point baskets in a NCAA Tournament regional game was 14. At the end of the first half, Michigan and North Carolina had combined for 13. By game's end, gunners in two shades of blue would team up to try 40 3-pointers—and make 20 of them.

But in the heart of horse country, the Heels had chosen the wrong weapons for a duel that was to become a battle of trifectas. As Fisher was to say later, "For Glen Rice, shooting a 3-pointer is like shooting a five-footer for you or me."

After Lebo played his pair of threes, Rice answered with one of his own to cut Carolina's lead to 26–21. With just under three minutes left in the half, North Carolina still owned a four-point lead. But Rice's fourth 3-pointer cut the Tar Heel's lead to 47–47. Then Mills capped a fast break with a layup to give Michigan the lead, 48–47, at the two-minute mark.

Both teams went cold for the rest of the half, combining to miss their next four shots. North Carolina had the chance for a last shot, but missed and Michigan rebounded. With time running out, Robinson raced the ball downcourt. Out of the corner of his eye he caught Rice streaking down the left side.

"I knew Rumeal saw me and I knew he'd get me the ball, so I ran the floor as hard as I could," Rice said later. "I really wanted to rip the rim out of the backboard, but I didn't quite do that."

Not quite. Nevertheless, Robinson's anticipation was perfect, and Rice's slam with two seconds left was awe-inspiring, if not backboard-shattering. The basket was still quivering as the Wolverines ran offcourt with a 50–47 halftime lead.

A Mills' turnaround put Michigan up by five to start the second half, and the Wolverines twice led by as many as six. But in a half that saw four lead changes and two ties, neither team was able to put the other away.

Fisher quieted Lebo by replacing Mike Griffin with Demetrius Calip. In the

Glen Rice was a senior co-captain who usually was content to let his play speak for itself.

first half, Lebo had treated Griffin as if he wasn't there, pouring in 17 points. In the second half, Lebo couldn't shake Calip, as the quick little sophomore held the Carolina senior to just two free throws after intermission.

On the inside Reid and Mills, who had been compared to each other ever since they were rated as the nation's top two high school stars, were going at each other with a vengeance. "I always like to play against J.R. because he's such a competitor," Mills had said. "I think the team that wants it worst will win," Reid had predicted. Both of these young men obviously wanted it badly. Reid, in what would prove to be his final college game, would finish with a team-high 26 points and six rebounds. Mills would end with 16 points, six rebounds, one assist, one block, and one steal.

Williams was suffering through the worst of his three games against Michigan. He would finish with only eight points. His counterpart Loy Vaught was continuing to struggle. Vaught, who had yet to play as well in the tournament as he had throughout the regular season, would take only three shots and finish with but four points before fouling out.

In the first half, North Carolina had done the unexpected by trying to beat Michigan in a shooting match. The Wolverines, hitting 58.9 percent of their shots, shot that strategy down. Realistically, the Tar Heels couldn't have shot much better than they did in the first segment. They knocked down 60.6 percent of their field goals—including 70 percent of their 3-point tries. Yet they trailed by three points. So it was back to the inside attack in the second half. With Reid, Williams, and forwards Steve Bucknall and Kevin Madden handling the scoring, the Tar Heels regained the lead at 57–56 with 15:21 remaining. When Reid canned a short turnaround from the right side, Carolina had a 59–56 lead with 14:35 left to play. But the die had been cast in the first half. North Carolina could do what it wanted. The Wolverines were content to keep bombing away. Twenty-six seconds later, Rice drilled a triple to tie the score.

Three-pointers by Rumeal Robinson and Sean Higgins pushed Michigan to a 74–68 lead with 9:42 remaining. North Carolina methodically pounded the ball inside and cut the margin to one with 6:18 left. Cue, Mr. Rice. His 3-pointer 25 seconds later made it 79–75 Michigan.

With 4:54 remaining, Lebo sank two free throws to pull North Carolina within two at 83–81. At the 4:07 mark, Reid powered in a line-drive turnaround from the right baseline, and it was an 83–83 game. Rice responded by dropping in a 21-footer from the right side. With 3:48 remaining, it was Michigan 86, North Carolina 83.

An inside basket by Williams and a free throw by Mark Huges left Michigan with an 87–85 lead at the two-minute mark. For 38 minutes, both teams had waged war. Once, Reid and Rice had pushed and shoved each other, almost breaking into a fight. For both teams, the stakes were high, the intensity higher. And with two minutes to go, the game was still within reach of both teams. It was coming down to the wire, and it was coming down to a battle between two college superstars, J.R. Reid and Glen Rice.

"I was thinking about North Carolina beating us twice," Rice said. "We weren't going to lose to North Carolina three times in three years. We didn't want to make an early exit again."

The Tar Heels, down by two points, had the ball. They worked it inside to Williams. He turned, fired, and missed. Rice rebounded with 1:44 showing on the clock. Forty-two seconds later, Rice rose up from the corner and dropped in a 3-pointer—his eighth of the game—and Michigan led, 90–85.

Carolina came right back, Reid hitting from inside to make it 90–87 with 50 seconds left. The Tar Heels wasted no time sending Robinson to the free throw stripe, and they got a chance to tie when he missed the front end of the bonus. But Reid's eight-footer was off, Higgins grabbed the rebound, and he made both free throws after the ensuing foul.

Final score: Michigan 92, North Carolina 87. The Wolverines had proven something, to their fans and themselves. "The Carolina game was very crucial because of the fact they had beaten us twice before," said assistant coach Mike Boyd. "It was like Dean Smith and Carolina blue had a jinx on Michigan. It was hard to believe that three straight times in the tournament we would draw North Carolina. It was unbelievable. It was almost like they were the Dallas Cowboys, America's team, and we're a little school from up north that plays football but is not that strong in basketball. So winning that game was very important."

There was no doubt how the Wolverines had done it. Robinson had played his best game in some time, with 17 points, 13 assists, and five rebounds. Mills had also played well, and Higgins had added 14 points, three assists, one steal, and only one turnover. Calip had bounced off the bench to put the clamps on Lebo, and Hughes and Vaught had combined to grab 12 rebounds. But the game had belonged to Glen Rice.

Rice hit 13 of the 19 shots he took, including 8-of-12 from 3-point land. He also grabbed six rebounds, and had two assists and one steal.

"It was just unbelievable, the shots they were hitting," said Dean Smith. "We had an asterisk next to Glen Rice's name. We weren't supposed to give him any daylight. But he still killed us with those 3-pointers. He hit some great shots."

Of course, great is in the eye of the beholder. Not that Steve Fisher thought there was anything wrong with Rice's shots. It was just that, as Fisher said, "I've been around Glen too long to let anything he does surprise me. It's to the point now where I get mad at him when he misses. He's been such a great player, and so consistent for us, I expect him to make his shot all the time."

Why not? During a break in one practice during the regular season, Rice and Frieder were on the concourse level of Crisler Arena, more than a third

Glen Rice with his mother Ernestine.

of the way up the arena's seats, when Frieder jokingly challenged his ace to make a shot from there. Rice, who was far stronger than his lean frame showed, came so close that onlookers were amazed. So he tried again. And made it.

Clearly, such shooting was something special. Just as clearly, Fisher definitely recognized that. After the game, a reporter told Fisher: "Coach, you seemed to pull all the right strings tonight. You made key substitutions, called timeouts at the right times, you really coached a fine game." Fisher looked at the guy as if he were from Venus. "You're nuts," he replied. "All I did was go out there and say, 'Get the ball to Glen Rice.' Glen Rice would make any coach look good."

Dean Smith wasn't about to argue. "I've never seen anything like that," he said. "I just can't believe he could come back and do that again tomorrow."

Perhaps the longtime North Carolina coach should've had more faith. Glen Rice certainly did. He was asked once how he stayed so calm and confident while shooting, no matter how difficult or important the shot was. "I don't worry," Rice said. "I just put the ball in the air. God takes it from there."

"This Is What Every Kid Dreams About"

Sean Higgins might not have had God helping him with his shot, but he did have the support of someone almost as powerful: Bo Schembechler.

One of the more unlikely sidelights of Michigan's 1989 NCAA Tournament run was the relationship that developed between Schembechler and Higgins, a 6–9 sophomore swingman from Los Angeles. At first blush, chances of the gruff coach taking Higgins under his wing would not seem very great. Higgins could play, especially on the offensive end, there was no doubt about that. But he was a flashy, undisciplined player. He had come to Michigan under something of a cloud, having first signed with UCLA and then petitioning the NCAA to void that signing, saying his stepfather had forced him to commit to the Bruins. His story was featured in *Sports Illustrated*, the NCAA voided his letter of intent, and he enrolled at Michigan. During his freshman year, Higgins lost his academic eligibility for the second semester, then drew assault charges for getting into a fight on a campus basketball court. He improved his grades for his sophomore year but, midway through that season, was suspended for three games when he broke team rules regarding drinking.

Not exactly the kind of guy you'd expect Schembechler to like. Yet Schembechler had always appreciated players who had what he called "moxie," and there was no doubt that Higgins possessed that quality in abundance—when he wanted to. As the NCAA Tournament unfolded, Schembechler seemed to develop a special fondness for Higgins. At the season-ending team banquet, Schembechler praised all of the regulars individually. But his favorite, he said, "is this Sean Higgins. He's going to be a great player—or I'm going to get him."

As Higgins discovered, being taken under Schembechler's wing wasn't like being clucked over by a mother hen. Schembechler liked Higgins because he saw him as a bright, extremely talented young player. But, for some reason, Higgins just wasn't playing nearly as well as he should have been. Even worse, it looked to Schembechler as if Higgins wasn't playing nearly as hard as he should have. To Schembechler, that was the cardinal sin. As he sat in The Omni watching Higgins go through the motions in Michigan's wins over Xavier and South Alabama, Schembechler shook his head and muttered to himself.

Back in Ann Arbor, Schembechler opened his Monday newspapers to see Higgins quoted in one paper as saying the players should be consulted on choosing the next head coach, and that he favored Cazzie Russell. In another paper, Higgins was quoted as saying that if Michigan's new coach wasn't to his liking, he would either transfer or turn pro. Schembechler shook his head and muttered some more. "We didn't need to be reading that stuff when we were going for the national title, for God's sake," Schembechler would recall later.

So when Steve Fisher asked Schembechler to speak to the team again before it left for the regionals at Lexington, Schembechler warned him, "Maybe I shouldn't. I may say something up there that might cost you a player."

"What do you mean?" Fisher asked.

Schembechler told him his thoughts on Higgins. "It's hard for me to accept a tremendously talented kid playing like he's playing. I'd have to say something."

"Well," Fisher said, "that's fine with me."

Shortly before the Wolverines left for their charter flight, Schembechler stood before them as they sat in courtside seats inside Crisler Arena.

"All right men, do you want to win this championship?" Schembechler said. "Rice, you've got to score 30 points. You other guys have got to make sure he gets 30 a game. You've got to get him the ball, set him up and let him shoot. Mills over there, you've got to knock 'em around in the paint and get down in there and get the job done. Rumeal, you're the best guard in the country. You've just got to play like it. Loy Vaught, you've been short-arming your shots. Hey, man, you've got to relax. You can rebound with anyone in the country. You and Hughes gotta go in there and be powerful guys in there. Do the job. Calip, you've got to keep coming off the bench and delivering like you have been. . . . "

One by one, Schembechler addressed the Wolverine regulars. He saved Higgins for last.

"Higgins, I wanta tell you something," Schembechler began. "I want you to know there isn't anybody here who gives a damn what you do three weeks from now or four weeks from now or a year from now or two years from now. You wanta leave here? Your goddamn transfer letter is on my desk. You can go get it right now before you get on the bus to go to Lexington. We're not gonna put up with that stuff around here. You either join this team or get out."

Schembechler paused, but only for an instant. "The next thing I want to tell you is, if you go down there, you start diving for those loose balls. You hustle all the time you're down there. And when you're substituted for, you don't walk off the floor, you run to your coach. You hear what he has to say and then sit down, and get in the ball game and get ready to play."

Moments later, Schembechler left. Higgins' jaw was still on the floor. "The look on his face was unbelievable," Mark Hughes recalled later. "I'm sure no one had ever talked to Sean like that before."

Bill Frieder had tried talking to Higgins in various ways. But he was never fully satisfied with the results. He was never really sure he was getting through. As the season wore on, it was easy to tell from Frieder's off-the-cuff and off-the-record comments that he had lost a lot of faith in Higgins.

Meanwhile, Higgins wasn't exactly thrilled at the way things were going for him in his first full season. "I feel like I should be starting," Higgins said between Michigan's first and second-round games in Atlanta. "I was starting, then I lost my starting job, and nobody ever told me why. Coach Frieder never talked to me about it."

Certainly, Higgins had the talent to start for virtually any team in the country. A slender 6–9, he could hit from long range like Glen Rice and handle the ball like a guard. Although not as bulky or strong as Michigan's other frontliners, he was a decent rebounder. With his combination of height and ballhandling, Higgins had occasional moments when he resembled Earvin "Magic" Johnson, one of his boyhood idols while growing up in L.A. But there were also moments when he resembled another idol—his father, Earle.

In 1963, Earle Higgins moved from Cincinnati to live with his grandparents in Ann Arbor. In 1965–66, the 6–7 Higgins led Ann Arbor High to the state finals, averaged 23 points per game, and broke three fiberglass backboards. More than 250 colleges came courting. Higgins wanted to stay in Ann Arbor and play for Michigan. Coach Dave Strack would have loved to have had him, but Higgins' grades weren't good enough. Strack helped him enroll in a junior college in Wyoming, but Higgins ended up transferring to Eastern Michigan University, in Ann Arbor's neighboring city of Ypsilanti. Higgins was a star at EMU, a star who went on to play for two years with the Indiana Pacers during the heyday of the American Basketball Association, before becoming an executive with Chrysler and settling in the Detroit suburbs.

That settling process took a while. In his early years, things didn't go as well for Earle Higgins off the basketball court. He got into scrapes with the law in both Wyoming and Michigan. Once, a judge briefly banned him from playing basketball. His marriage broke up. Sean lived in Ann Arbor for the first 10 years of his life, but then he moved with his mother to Los Angeles.

That separation couldn't sever the bonds between father and son. As Sean Higgins developed into a McDonald's All-America in high school, Frieder courted him assiduously, with Earle Higgins' blessing. He wanted Sean to attend Michigan. It would be a reunion for father and son, and Sean could be close to his sister Jamie, who had already enrolled at Michigan. And Earle

Higgins, who had dreamed of playing for Michigan, could see his old number, 24, worn on the maize and blue jersey of his son.

Over the years, father and son played a lot of driveway basketball. As Sean grew older, those games increasingly made Earle Higgins feel as if he were trying to guard his reflection in a mirror.

Michigan assistant coach Mike Boyd, who played for Northern Michigan against Earle and later helped the Wolverines recruit Sean, said: "Earle looked a lot like Sean out there and he played a lot like Sean, except Earle was more of an inside player."

Over the years, the games between Earle and Sean Higgins became more competitive. But Earle, 21 years older and wiser, always won. Until Sean's senior year in high school, on the weekend he made his official visit to Michigan. "Luckily, I had an excuse, that I was in my street shoes," Earle Higgins recalled. "It was uncanny. He doesn't miss. You play 'make it, keep it' with him and you never see the ball. That told me he had arrived. It also told me I was out of shape, but it made me feel good, too. I enjoy watching Sean play. It's like watching myself on film. Except I didn't shoot as much."

Shooting was definitely something Sean Higgins didn't shy away from. A scout who saw him in high school dubbed Higgins the Will Rogers of West Coast basketball "because he never met a shot he didn't like." Frieder, who would readily pull a player out of a game for taking bad shots, nicknamed him "Trigger." Through his aborted freshman year and most of his sophomore season, Higgins lived up to both labels pretty well. When it came to shooting, he had no conscience. Higgins would fire it up any time, from anywhere. Surprisingly, he blended in with the Wolverines far better than many had thought he would. He made sure he got his shots, but he didn't play selfishly. The trouble was, he often didn't shoot intelligently. He would fire up quick bombs when the situation called for patiently pounding the ball inside. In the first part of his sophomore year that didn't matter much because Michigan was so much better than most of the teams it played. But as competition got tighter during the Big Ten season, a bad shot or two by Higgins, or anybody, could cost a game.

Higgins also did not play defensively. At least not very well, not very often. He was a liability at the defensive end, especially when he played guard and tried to contain smaller men out on the perimeter. That had been one of Frieder's prime concerns entering the season, and he felt it was proving true as the season progressed. He had wanted to use Higgins at the off-guard, which would allow him to start a front line of Rice, Mills, and Vaught or Hughes. Having the 6–9 Higgins and the 6–7 Rice on opposite wings to bomb away over opposing defenses was an enticing prospect. But Frieder feared that Higgins wasn't yet a good enough ballhandler or defender to be a quality Big Ten guard. When Higgins and the rest of Michigan's backcourt misfired in early Big Ten losses to Illinois, Wisconsin, and Indiana, Frieder decided his

At 6-9, Sean Higgins had all the tools to be an outstanding player.

fears had been justified. He began to make more use of Mike Griffin, Kirk Taylor, and then Demetrius Calip in the backcourt.

Meanwhile, Michigan coaches and players were often left to shake their heads at Higgins' offcourt behavior. When he became academically ineligible midway through his freshman year, it wasn't because he wasn't smart enough. And the class in which he got his decisive low grade was speech, a class that should have been a lock for someone as outgoing and bright as Higgins. In fact, his work for the class was solid. The trouble was, Higgins didn't go to class regularly, and his final grade was based partly on attendance. Later Higgins would confess, "You know in high school when you're a basketball player, sometimes they'll go a little easier on your grades or tests. I kinda thought it would be the same here, but I found out that it's not. The only thing it's going to take for Sean Higgins to be successful at Michigan is for Sean Higgins to get his big butt out of bed."

By late December of his freshman year, Higgins and Michigan coaches knew his grades were borderline. Waiting to find out his fate "was like hanging from the Empire State Building," Higgins would say later, "and I fell. And it hurt." As Higgins waited, the team was playing at a Christmas tournament in Tampa. Adjoining the hotel where the team stayed was a disco. On an off night, Higgins—who was underage—and some teammates visited the bar. Higgins nearly got into a fight and the police were summoned. Utilizing a little Southern hospitality, they only gave Higgins a warning. One week later, on the day Michigan was to open its Big Ten season at Northwestern, Higgins was declared ineligible. At the time, Frieder downplayed the loss of Higgins, who had averaged 10 points off the bench and had been Michigan's leading 3-point shooter in pre-conference games. But later, the coach would admit that losing Higgins probably cost the Wolverines two or three games—a total that might have boosted them from second place in the Big Ten to first, or might have resulted in a longer run in the NCAA Tournament. Frieder responded to Higgins' grade problems by telling him to stay away from practice and concentrate on his studies. So Higgins played his basketball at campus recreation facilities. It was at one of those where, a few weeks later, he was involved in a fight that led to an assault charge against him. Somewhat reluctantly, Frieder decided it would be better to have Higgins practicing with the team than to set him loose among the general public.

It seemed that Higgins just couldn't stay away from controversy. In late December of Higgins' sophomore season, after a crushing victory over Northern Michigan that was the Wolverines' last game before their Christmas break, Higgins joined teammates in celebrating Terry Mills' birthday. But Higgins celebrated longer and harder than he should have, and while driving later that night he was pulled over by police. Higgins was charged with impaired driving. Frieder responded by suspending Higgins for three games, both of the games Michigan would play in the Utah Classic and Michigan's Big Ten opener against Northwestern. Playing without Higgins for the first time against Alaska-Anchorage in the Utah Classic opener, the Wolverines suffered their first loss of the season.

(It was during the Alaska-Anchorage game that another of the Wolverines' themes emerged. As the Seawolves closed in on the upset, some of their players kept firing each other up by saying, "We're going to shock the world!" At the time, the Michigan players chuckled at the gung-ho Seawolves. Later they incorporated that phrase into their own battle cry, going "on a mission to shock the world.")

Although they had every right to be angry with Higgins, his teammates stuck by him. "He's not a bad guy," Rumeal Robinson said. "Sean's just Sean." Later in the season, when Higgins' transfer talk hit the fan after Michigan's first two NCAA Tournament wins, his teammates remained in his corner. "We knew he wasn't a bad guy at all," Mills said. "Some people don't realize how hard it is to go from high school, where you're almost always the most talented player, to college, where all of a sudden there are a lot of good players. It gets frustrating sometimes. Me and Sean both got to that point at one time or another. We blamed Frieder for it. After you hear from enough people that your coach is holding you back, you start wondering yourself. You get frustrated, and you think about going somewhere else. I think it happens to just about everybody. But everybody can't score 30 each game, and after a while you finally realize that. Plus we didn't pay it too much attention because it was Sean talking, and Sean has so much hot air. A week later, after he scored 30 against Virginia, he was saying he wanted to build a house in Ann Arbor."

Michigan's regional final game against Virginia was the one in which Sean Higgins burst into the public eye. But his breakthrough came one game before, against North Carolina. He scored 14 points, had two rebounds, three assists, one steal, and just one turnover. In the closing seconds of the game, he came up with a rebound and two free throws that clinched the victory. More significantly, Higgins looked like a different player. To Schembechler, who couldn't be at the game in person because he had to testify in the Chicago trial of two sports agents, the difference was apparent on his TV screen. "I remember there was a loose ball bouncing over to the sidelines and all of a sudden, here comes this Michigan blur into the picture, going after the ball," Schembechler grinned. "And it was Higgins! After the game was over, I called Steve to congratulate him and I made a point to ask him to tell Higgins that I thought he had played a helluva game. I don't think I can take any credit for that. I think I just woke him up, then Steve took over and did a good job working with him."

But Michigan professor Howard Brabson, who had become a confidant of

Some of Sean Higgins' decisions—both oncourt and off—did not make Bill Frieder smile.

many players through his work overseeing the university's mentor program for athletes, said Schembechler underestimated his impact. Of Higgins' reaction to Schembechler's pep talk, Brabson said: "This young man said, in essence, that was the first time a coach had really paid enough attention to him to point out his flaws. His perspective of it was a very positive one, that it meant somebody cared. From there on in, Sean got better in a lot of ways. His grades went up, his behavior changed. We began to see him grow from a California playboy who came here thinking he was God's gift to basketball into a kid who's now beginning to look at it as 'I'm a kid who plays on a team.'"

That growth began to become apparent at Lexington, and not just on the court. "We've been trying to tell Sean to let his play on the court do his talking, and to watch what he says off it," said Fisher. On the Friday between games, when Higgins was one of the Michigan players sent to the NCAA-mandated press conference, he showed he was learning what his coaches meant. His performance was impressive, as much for what he didn't say as for what he did. This was Kentucky, after all, where coach Eddie Sutton had just resigned, where most of the citizens of the Commonwealth were waiting anxiously to see what sanctions the NCAA would levy against the Wildcats, and where, two years before, Higgins had visited as a highly regarded recruiting target, one who had been interviewed in the subsequent NCAA investigation. Reporters, especially those from Lexington, peppered him with questions about the NCAA investigation and Kentucky's efforts to recruit him. Time after time, Higgins fended them off deftly, saying it wasn't the time for him to comment.

But Sean also remained Sean, treating reporters to several good lines and winning many of them over with his outgoing, boyish charm. At the end of the press conference, the Wolverines marked Fisher's 44th birthday by presenting him with a cake, and telling him to make a wish and blow out the candles. "You guys help me," said Fisher, moving the cake toward his players. "You know how it is when you turn 44," Higgins told reporters. "You lose your wind." A reporter asked Higgins if he would return to Michigan if Fisher were named head coach. "I'll be at Michigan next season regardless, whether the coach is Steve Fisher or Elmer Fudd," Higgins replied. Then there was Higgins, telling about the Wolverines' visit the day before to one of the area's thoroughbred horse farms. "We thought it was going to be kind of boring, but once we got there it was kind of interesting," said Higgins. "There was this horse, Alydar, and they told us about all the sex he gets, and that was really interesting. They told us about how much he gets for stud service. They said he gets $300,000 every time. If I was getting that, I'd be a rich man."

The next day, Michigan played Virginia for the right to advance to the Final

Four. Higgins shot as if he were not only rich, but as if he owned the shooting bank. And so did Glen Rice.

Rice's teammates had long before hung the nickname "rain" on those times when Rice's sweet jumper was in an extra-special groove, when his shot just kept falling and falling. This Saturday afternoon was just such a time. The tone was set immediately: Richard Morgan, Virginia's long-range counterpart to Rice, opened with a 3-point attempt that clanged off the rim. Rice came down and fired up a jumper. It swished cleanly through the net. So did his next shot. And his next. And . . . Rice hit his first six shots, and nine of his first 10. For the game, he canned 13-of-16 for a remarkable 81.3 field goal percentage—extraordinarily remarkable when you consider that many of those baskets came on mid-to-long range jumpers, including 4-of-5 from 3-point land. Rice finished with 32 points, the third straight game in which he had scored more than 30. "I've seen Rice two games in a row now, and I'd have to say he's as fine an offensive player as I've seen in a long, long time," said Virginia coach Terry Holland.

Then there was Higgins. When he first entered the game as a substitute for Rice, Michigan already owned an 11–5 lead. Rice had scored nine of those points, and the Cavaliers had to be glad to see him head for the bench. But it took Higgins less than 30 seconds to hit his first shot. One minute later, he hit his second. After one more minute, he nailed his first 3-pointer of the day and it was 18–7 Michigan.

Now Rice was back in the game, this time along with Higgins. The long-distance bucket brigade that Frieder and his staff had dreamed of was about to become reality. Rice followed Higgins' first triple with two of his own, and Michigan owned a 24–12 lead. Virginia cut the margin to 24–17. Then Michigan went on a tear, hitting five straight baskets, two by Rumeal Robinson. With 4:22 remaining in the half, it was a 34–17 game and it was quickly becoming crystal clear that this was the Wolverines' day.

Michigan owned a 44–25 halftime lead that it just kept expanding early in the second half. It was 65–40 with 12:13 remaining. That's when Higgins really went to work. He hit a 3-pointer from the right side, then after a Rice basket, nailed a triple from the left baseline to make it 73–40 Michigan. With 7:20 remaining, Higgins drilled a triple from the top of the key. One minute later, he took a Robinson pass on the left side, spun, and sank a 20-foot turn-around for three. Just 15 seconds later, he nailed another three from the left wing, and Michigan led, 89–54.

When the smoke finally cleared, Higgins had finished with a career-high 31 points. He had made good on 11-of-15 field goal tries, including 7-of-10 3-pointers. At one stretch, he hit six straight triples. His total of seven tied the record for a regional game.

"I wish I could have had the same fire in my eyes that Higgins had in his," said Virginia forward Bryant Stith. "They shot the ball with so much confidence that it really took the steam out of us."

Said Virginia's other starting forward, Matt Blundin: "Even our easy shots weren't going in, and it seemed like they didn't miss a shot."

"I could tell after I took my first shot that I was back in that groove," said Rice, named the Most Outstanding Player of the Southeast Regional.

"I felt like I was the best player on the court, like there wasn't anything I couldn't do," said Higgins.

Said Virginia's Morgan: "I kind of figured the odds would come around and they would start to miss a few. But it seemed like whenever Rice would miss, Higgins would be there on the other side to throw it in. It was like they were trading threes back and forth. It was very frustrating."

There was no frustration for the Wolverines. For them, it was sheer jubilation. As he sat on the sidelines waiting for the game to end, Higgins was so pumped up that assistant coach Mike Boyd had to step over to him and tell him to calm down. When the final horn sounded, Higgins grabbed the game ball and threw it into the Michigan cheering section, just over Angie Fisher's head. Moments later, the Wolverines cut down the victory net, symbolically saving the last strand for Fisher, who trimmed it while a large and vocal contingent of Michigan fans chanted, "Fisher, Fisher."

Michigan had claimed a 102–65 victory. Along with Rice, Higgins and Robinson had been named to the regional's all-tournament team. The win set a slew of Michigan records, including the largest victory margin ever recorded by a Michigan team in NCAA Tournament play. Most importantly, Michigan was going to the Final Four for the first time in 13 years. "This is what every kid dreams about," Higgins said. "It's what I've been playing all my life for. And we're going!"

They were heady moments, indeed. Even guard Marc Koenig, who had been picked by Dick Vitale for his "All-Walk-on Team," walked away with the very special memories that come from playing the last minute of a record-setting rout. "I was just so hyper, so happy to be in there," Koenig explained. "I wanted to get my name on the stat sheet, but I think I was too nervous to shoot the ball, so I stole a pass. Then three Virginia guys closed in on me and I thought, 'Wait a minute, What am I doing here?' I watch all the films, too, so when their point guard held up one hand and called for the 'C play,' I knew just what they were going to run. I turned around and yelled at the guys, 'Chicago! They're going to run Chicago!' And they're all looking at me like, 'What do we care?'"

Schembechler, who had flown down for the game, was asked before it started whether Michigan would name a new head coach after the tournament ended or after the Wolverines had been eliminated. "After the tournament, period," he said, "because we will be involved in the tournament until the very end."

After Michigan overwhelmed Virginia, Cavaliers forward Bryant Stith said: "I wish I could've had the fire in my eyes that Sean Higgins did when he was shooting."

After the game, he went into the Michigan lockerroom to give the players a few brief but typically rousing remarks. "Men, I think you know now that you have what it takes to win this whole damn thing," Schembechler said. "And you know what I hope? I hope you get Illinois."

The next day, the Fighting Illini slipped past Syracuse to win their regional. The rematch was set. It would be Michigan against Illinois in one of the following Saturday's national semifinal games. On Monday, Fisher walked into Schembechler's office. "Well, we got what you wished for," Fisher said. "Now what am I supposed to do with them?"

"We're a Totally Different Team Now"

The Final Four. The dream of every schoolboy basketball player, the Holy Grail for every Division I coach, the March Madness mania that grew and grew during the 1980s until it became one of America's premier sporting events, on a par with the World Series and the Super Bowl. The Final Four. The ultimate goal, the ultimate test. For most people who ever reach it, a once-in-a-lifetime experience. And now, the Michigan Wolverines were there. On the door of equipment manager Bob Bland, only two pieces of the national championship puzzle remained covered.

During the stretch run of Michigan's regular season, as the Wolverines embarked upon their "mission," coach Bill Frieder said several times that his team's goal was to keep winning and winning, until it could gain a NCAA Tournament rematch with "that other team"—meaning Indiana, which had handed the Wolverines those two stinging defeats. In the next few weeks, the Wolverines accomplished enough to set the stage for Frieder's scenario. But ironically, as Final Four week began to unfold, Frieder wasn't around to enjoy the results. And neither was Indiana. The Hoosiers were upset in the West Regional semifinal by Seton Hall, which went on to trip Nevada–Las Vegas for one Final Four berth. The Pirates would meet Duke, winner of the East Regional, in the first of Saturday afternoon's national championship semifinals in the Seattle Kingdome.

For the Michigan Wolverines, it would be a Final Four in which irony had a starring role. The Wolverines would get their Big Ten rematch, all right. But instead of Indiana, it would be with Illinois, the only team that had hung two decisive defeats on Michigan during the regular season. Steve Fisher, who had become the Cinderella character of the NCAA Tournament, would be pitted against Illinois coach Lou Henson. The week before, Fisher had beaten North Carolina's legendary Dean Smith. Now he would go against Henson, one of college basketball's winningest coaches and a man who, several years earlier, had come close to hiring Fisher as an assistant at Illinois.

To the fans on the outside, the Final Four is a tremendous happening, an exciting, emotion-packed, three-game long weekend that is the epitome of college basketball. To those on the inside, the players and coaches, it is a tension-filled pressure cooker. The tournament that had begun with 64 hopeful teams was down to four, and in Seattle, those four teams would find themselves descended upon, besieged, questioned, and dissected by over 800 reporters. For players like Glen Rice, still a reluctant interview subject, there would be no place to hide. Not only did the NCAA require teams to open their postgame lockerrooms, it ordered teams to hold press conferences and to make more and more players available to the press as teams advanced. Even players who were used to dealing with the press would be subjected to a media microscope unlike anything they had ever experienced. For Michigan, this is where another ironic factor clicked in: Frieder's untimely departure had the unintended and unexpected benefit of preparing the Wolverines for the Final Four's media onslaught. "I think it may have been a blessing in disguise," said Mark Hughes. "Because of Coach Frieder leaving, the media were all over us right from the beginning. Before the Xavier game, they were asking all kinds of questions, but almost none of them had anything to do with Xavier. We were getting the kind of attention that teams don't usually get until they get to the Final Four. As we moved on, it actually got easier to deal with instead of the other way around."

Media pressure wasn't the only kind being exerted upon Michigan basketball as Final Four week began. With each win, public pressure built for Bo Schembechler to name Fisher as Michigan's new head coach. While reporters repeatedly asked Schembechler and Fisher about the coaching job, letters supporting Fisher poured into Schembechler's office. After Michigan's first two tourney wins, the *Ann Arbor News* asked readers to phone in their choice for new head coach. Overwhelmingly, they favored Fisher, and that support only intensified after he led the Wolverines to two more wins. After Michigan beat Virginia in the regional finals, Frieder said from Arizona that it was "appalling" that Schembechler hadn't already given the job to Fisher. More and more columnists and commentators called for Fisher's appointment, and wondered why Schembechler was taking so long to make what seemed like an obvious decision.

Fisher and Schembechler handled the questions with the same stock answers. "I told Steve when all this started that we would sit down and talk after the tournament, and that's what we're going to do," Schembechler said. "Right now I'm just concentrating on the task at hand," said Fisher. "Given what has happened, I think Steve Fisher will be a head coach somewhere next season. I hope it will be at Michigan, but we'll just have to wait and see about that."

In the meantime, Fisher's life had changed dramatically. During a press conference the Monday before the Final Four, he talked about how he had scrambled around the year before to get a Final Four ticket for his wife, Angie. He told how he finally wound up getting her a seat close to Bobbi Olsen, wife of Arizona coach Lute Olsen, whose Wildcats were eliminated in a semifinal game. "She sat there looking at Bobbi Olsen and she said later that she just couldn't fathom what that would be like, to sit there and watch your husband coach in the Final Four," Fisher said. "Life twists and turns in funny ways."

For the Fishers, there had been all kinds of ironic twists. Until the previous Christmas, they had never owned a telephone answering machine. Then they both decided they needed one. On Christmas morning, they discovered they had both bought machines as gifts for each other. They took one back and kept the other, to use when they were on vacation and "number one, so we could turn it on at dinnertime and have some family time," Fisher said. Now, Fisher found himself using the machine most of the time. "The phone last night . . . rang non-stop, and in about a 20-minute span it was never over 20 seconds before it rang again. We just had to put the recorder on, and my wife took off 23 messages when she finally backed it up. I never thought I'd be the kind of guy who'd sit there and listen as people called in and got the recorder. Sometimes I feel guilty not picking up the phone. But I'm trying to do what I've told the kids to do, prioritize and focus on the task at hand." While he was prioritizing, Fisher's answering machine was, indeed, getting quite a workout. Among those calling were "two or three guys I played ball with that I hadn't seen in 15 years. And I've had telegrams from former classmates."

Growing up in the southern Illinois town of Herrin, Fisher had been, like all those around him, a Fighting Illini fan. Now he had become a hometown hero who would lead his team against his former favorites. "That's a little town of about 9,000 people, so you can imagine the celebrity status my family is feeling now," Fisher said. "The TV station from about 50 miles away came and wanted to interview my father, but he wouldn't let them in. But both my brothers are talking to anyone who wants to talk to them."

Fisher wasn't the only one who had to cope with sudden celebrity. Stopping in an Ann Arbor store, Koenig found himself fawned over by fans who told him how lucky he was to be going to the Final Four. Overhearing this talk, a man walked over to Koenig. "Going to the Final Four, eh?" the man asked Koenig. "Yep," smiled the walk-on. "So, are you in the band or what?" asked the fan.

Things didn't change much when the scene switched to Seattle at midweek. "I got up early this morning to go over and pick up my credentials and a couple of tickets that were waiting for me," Fisher said. "Boy, did I find out what the Final Four is all about. I got caught in a deluge of friends and other people who wanted to chat or do an interview with me, or who wanted tickets. You know, I've experienced this as an outsider looking in for the last 10

Happiness is moving on to the Final Four: Sean Higgins (24) and Terry Mills (52) savor the victory over Virginia.

Steve Fisher was learning to cope with being in the spotlight, even when a CBS-TV announcer introduced him after the win over Virginia as "Steve Frieder." Looking on are Demetrius Calip, Marc Koenig, Terry Mills, Sean Higgins, Eric Riley, Glen Rice, James Voskuil, and Mark and Angie Fisher.

years. This is a whole lot different. And I don't think I want to go back to being on the outside."

Fisher may have been a newcomer to college basketball's showcase event, but he was handling himself like a veteran. During a teleconference press session featuring all of the Final Four coaches, Henson said that although forward Ken Battle and center Lowell Hamilton were both nursing injuries, he expected both to play. Then Fisher was asked about the Wolverines' physical status. "We're fine," he said, "but in the interest of the good health of both Ken Battle and Lowell Hamilton, I suggest that Coach Henson keep them out of action for at least another week." Nevertheless, Fisher was beginning to feel the pressure. "I think I've been a bit more edgy here than I was in either Atlanta or Lexington," he admitted. "I mean, yesterday I was looking for things to get mad about."

If Fisher, or the Wolverines, really needed anything to get mad about, all they had to do was look back at tapes of their first two games against Illinois. There was more than enough there to arouse anger—or worry. The Illini hadn't handled the Wolverines in those two games, they had manhandled them, dusting them off with ease both times. "We've seen Illinois up close and personal twice this season, and we know firsthand what a great team they are," Fisher said. "Illinois is a great, great basketball team, maybe the best in the country with the overall speed and quickness they have. Quickness was a critical factor in those first two games. We didn't have it and they beat us to death with it. I remember in Crisler when they beat us in that last game, they beat us to every loose ball. We'd shoot and miss, it'd look like we were going to get it, and Nick Anderson or somebody would sprint right past us and get it."

Quickness wasn't all Illinois had going for it. Lacking a true center in the classic big man sense, the Illini had no regular over 6–8. But they also had no regular under 6–4, and most of the Illini stood at 6–6 or 6–7. Because all their players possessed quickness and fine jumping ability, this wasn't the handicap it seemed it might be. In fact, the Illini—whom *Sports Illustrated* dubbed the "Positionless Clones"—turned it to their advantage by playing a rugged man-to-man defense that emphasized switching every time opponents tried to set screens. Beat one Illinois defender, or get a pick from a teammate, and you were likely to find yourself guarded by another Illini who looked and played just like the last one. "It makes it hard because our offense is built around setting a lot of screens for Glen," said Loy Vaught, "but that just isn't as effective when the other team switches every time. And you can't really work for mismatches because they're all the same size."

Defending against the identical Illini could be frustrating, too. In fact, some players said that, in the heat of the game, it was sometimes hard to figure out which of the "PCs" they were supposed to guard or block out on rebounds. If Illinois was a team of average 6–7 players, that might not have mattered quite so much. But these were the Flying Illini, who not only jumped very well but threw themselves at the boards with reckless abandon. Especially Battle and Anderson, who loved to demoralize opponents by snatching away offensive rebounds and throwing down powerful slam dunks. So good was Illinois' offensive rebounding that some sportswriters suggested that the Illini's best offense was a missed shot.

Then there was the Gill Factor. A sometime starter the year before, 6–4 junior Kendall Gill had transformed himself into a wondrous player through an off-season devoted to lifting weights and practicing his outside shooting. Not only did he give Illinois exceptional defense and the long-range threat it had lacked before, but he gave the Illini a spirited on-court leader who seemed to have a knack for coming up with big plays. When he broke a bone in his left foot against Georgia Tech, Illinois was 17–0 and ranked No. 1 in the country. Without Gill, the Illini went 8–4 in their next 12 games. Then he returned, and Illinois reeled off six straight wins. With Gill in the lineup, the Illini were 23–0. No wonder some writers had begun calling them Gillinois. "Illinois is a terrific basketball team with or without Kendall Gill," noted Fisher, "but they might be sensational with him."

But if Illinois was a different team with Gill, Michigan was a different team with Fisher. "I think we may possibly have the edge," said Demetrius Calip, "because they may be expecting the team they beat twice, but we're a totally different team now. We're no longer playing not to lose. Now we're playing to win. Before when you went in, if you made a turnover you knew you would come right back out. I think that fear is what held us back. Now we're going in with the confidence factor."

Said Vaught: "We're definitely a different team because our confidence level is way, way up. I like to call Fisher, 'Mr. Psychologist.' He knows how to get into the mental aspect of a guy's game better than Frieder did. At the tail end of the season under Coach Frieder we were playing a little lethargic. Now we're playing harder, and I think that's because Coach Fisher allows us a little more freedom, and he's more of a people person. After that last Illinois game we felt bad, but we felt that we had worked hard, and that day we just got beat by a better team. But we now feel we're playing up to their level and maybe beyond that."

If Michigan was to beat Illinois in the Final Four, one player who would have to play at a higher level was Mike Griffin, the 6–7 junior who had grown up in suburban Chicago. In the first two games against Illinois, Gill had made Griffin look like he was wearing cement sneakers. Nevertheless, he would be given the task of checking Gill once again. Griffin was the Wolverines' best defender, and his size could be an advantage. If he couldn't do the job, the Wolverines would probably have to turn to Calip, the 6–1 sophomore who was solid defensively but lacked Griffin's size and experience.

Among the Wolverines, Griffin was an anomaly. On a team of quick draw

Mike Griffin, pictured playing against Northwestern, would be a key figure in Michigan's Final Four game with Illinois.

sharpshooters, Griffin was the guy who kept his weapon holstered. Whole games would go by without Griffin taking even one shot; in fact, in the Final Four, Griffin would start both games, play nearly half of each, and yet not score a single point, taking only one shot. During the regular season, Crisler Arena fans got so impatient with Griffin for continually passing up open shots that they once chanted, "Shoot, shoot," when he was preparing to take a foul shot. But Griffin, who had averaged 24.5 points on 58 percent shooting in high school, knew his role. And he was the kind of young man who could take selflessness to a new level. "An open 15-footer by me may not be the best shot for our team, not when I can get it to Glen Rice for an eight-foot shot," Griffin said. If Michigan fans sometimes didn't appreciate Griffin's willingness to role-play, Michigan coaches did. Like hockey coaches, they kept extensive plus-minus statistics for every player. And they knew that the player with the best plus-minus ratio on the team, the guy who was in on more wins than anybody, was Griffin.

The problem against Illinois would be how to get Griffin to play his role against Gill better than he ever had. For the answer, the Wolverines turned to a little dose of high technology.

Throughout Bill Frieder's tenure as head coach, Michigan had made as much, if not more, use of videotape than any college team in the country. The Wolverines owned enough VCRs to start a dealership, they had a satellite dish, and managers were constantly taping and trading for film on almost every possible opponent. By the time the NCAA Tournament rolled around, Michigan annually had tapes on nearly every team picked for the tourney. As Frieder's assistant, one of Fisher's prime responsibilities had been to "break down" those films, choosing which bits and pieces were needed to illustrate points the coaching staff wanted to emphasize.

Since Frieder's departure, that task had fallen to assistant coaches Mike Boyd, Brian Dutcher, and Joe "Smoke" Czupek, helping increase the workload on a coaching staff that was one body short. Partly to ease that strain and partly in an effort to get any edge possible heading into the Final Four, Michigan retained the services of Mitch Cauffman, a former Wolverines' manager who had gone on to start a sports video company, Hoop One. For Cauffman, Final Four weekend would prove to be a mostly sleepless orgy of taping, editing, and dubbing, as he cranked out tape after tape in response to coaches' requests.

To prepare for Illinois, Michigan players watched tapes of the first two games as a group. Then Boyd and Dutcher held individual sessions with each player, studying specific plays and matchups. In addition, Boyd took Griffin and Sean Higgins aside to study a special tape he had ordered, one focusing on how Gill had played against Griffin in the teams' first two meetings. "When you get to the Final Four, you need an edge," Boyd said later. "I don't know whether that was it or not, but I do know that our kids got awfully tired of looking at videos."

By late Saturday afternoon, Gill was awfully tired of looking at Griffin. And Higgins. Griffin played Gill much more physically than he had previously, putting his body on him and denying him his favored spots on the floor. Higgins followed suit when he subbed for Griffin. They combined to limit Gill to 11 points—only four in the second half—and a mere two assists. The Illini's best long-distance dialer was held to just two 3-point tries, neither of which he made.

The Wolverines needed every bit of that defense. The Illini's Kenny Battle played a fierce game, hitting 10-of-17 field goals and 8-of-10 free throws for a game-high 29 points. Nick Anderson hit crucial shot after crucial shot for 17 points and Lowell Hamilton matched Gill's 11 tallies. Steve Bardo counted only seven points but dished off eight assists and grabbed six rebounds.

From the opening tip, it was a struggle that did the Big Ten proud. In the next 40 minutes, there would be 33 lead changes and seven ties. Illinois jumped out to its largest lead early, at 16–8. Michigan claimed its biggest bulge about four minutes into the second half, when a Higgins' follow shot put the Wolverines up, 51–44.

With 8:40 remaining, Rumeal Robinson sank two free throws to give Michigan a 60–56 lead. Battle followed an Illini miss to cut the margin to two. Then Gill notched one of his three steals. He fed a driving Battle, who made the layup, drew a Terry Mills foul, and converted the 3-point play to put Illinois up, 61–60. From there on in, it was anybody's ball game.

With 3:25 left, Robinson hurried the ball downcourt, spotted Mark Hughes coming in hard from the right wing, and led him for a slam dunk that gave Michigan a 76–74 lead. On Illinois' next possession, Robinson stole the ball and fed Rice for a jam that put Michigan up, 78–74. Illinois called time with 3:01 showing.

The Illini worked the ball to Anderson, but he misfired from eight feet away. Mills rebounded but threw the ball away and Gill grabbed it. Bardo put up a 3-point try from the left side. It missed, but Battle chased the loose ball down in the right corner. Just as they had done so many times in the first two games, the Illini had beaten Michigan to the loose ball. Battle spun around and fired up an off-balance, 22-footer that kissed the glass and went in for three. With 2:28 left, Michigan's lead had dwindled to 78–77.

Rice got into the lane for an 11-foot jumper, but it missed and Gill rebounded. Bardo got the ball to Hamilton, who hit from the left baseline. Illinois 79, Michigan 78. With 1:36 remaining, Michigan called time.

The Wolverines came back out and worked the ball to Mills, who was in good position for one of his favorite shots, a jumper from the lane. He missed, but Hughes sliced toward the hoop like a runaway Mack truck. The senior co-captain grabbed the rebound and went right back up with it, putting up a soft seven-footer as Hamilton tried vainly for the block. Hughes' shot fell, and Hamilton was whistled for his fifth foul.

Assistant coach Mike Boyd spent much of his time off the floor overseeing the Wolverines' video preparations.

After Michigan had won, Terry Mills could joke about missing shots against the Fighting Illini.

"The shot went up and I saw it," Hughes said. "I tried to guess where it was going to come off and luckily I guessed right. I just got it and shot it back in. On the free throw, I wasn't thinking too much. I knew I was going to hit it. I had to. It was money time, a crunch situation."

Hughes hit the free throw cleanly. The Wolverines were beating the Illini at their own game, cashing in on offensive rebounds. Hughes' 3-point play gave the Wolverines an 81–79 lead with 1:09 remaining.

Nineteen seconds later, Illinois used its second timeout. As the Illini gathered around Henson, Fisher rallied his troops at the opposite bench. Flashing what Hughes would later call "a smile of confidence," the coach calmly laid out the Michigan strategy. He noted that, with 50 seconds left in the game and 26 seconds on the shot clock, the Wolverines would get another possession whether Illinois scored or not. Regardless of what happened, he said, he wasn't going to call another timeout. "I'm going to let you guys do it," he said, explaining what play they should try for the last shot. "I'm going to let you guys win it."

Later, Hughes would say, "We knew we were going to win at that point. That was a real confidence-builder to see him so composed, although I'm sure that inside he was going crazy."

Said Loy Vaught: "It was just what we needed. We were all hyped up. If we went out all hyped up there's no telling what would've happened. Someone probably would've thrown up a crazy shot. Instead, we went back out with confidence."

So did the Illini. They had been in this situation many times before, and they had risen to the occasion time after time. They had a 10-game winning streak and two previous victories over Michigan to bolster their confidence. Once again, they showed that confidence was not misplaced. Bardo got the ball to Battle and, with 30 seconds remaining, he nailed a 12-footer from the left side to make it an 81–81 game.

Down the floor came Robinson. He took the dribble to his left, looking for the designated play to develop. Mills and Hughes were to screen just off the lane for Rice and Higgins. But the Illini pressured and switched. Neither shooter could get open. Robinson kept his dribble and drove toward the left baseline, where he was sandwiched between a pair of Illinois defenders. Desperately, he looked for an open man. Finally, he saw Mills floating out on the right baseline. He flipped the ball toward the big center, but the pass was high and Mills had to retreat to haul it in.

Time was running out, and deja vu was taking over. This game was ending so much like the first loss to Indiana, when Mills had missed a 3-pointer from the right corner, then Hughes had rebounded and missed a short baseline jumper as time ran out.

Just as in that game, Mills went up from near the 3-point arc. Just as in that game, his shot drew iron and bounced off to the left. Just as in that game, a Michigan player came down with the rebound on the left baseline.

Steve Fisher en route to becoming the first rookie coach to win a national championship.

But this time it was, wonder of wonders, Higgins with the rebound. Higgins, who in the 32 games leading up to this one had a grand total of only 27 offensive rebounds. "Coach had been telling me all year that shots like that come off on the weak side, so I put myself in position for the rebound," Higgins said after the game.

Said Nick Anderson, who was caught under the basket as Higgins grabbed the ball: "I had him boxed out. The ball just bounced long. When I turned around, he was in the act of shooting, and I didn't want to foul him."

With two seconds left, Higgins went right back up with the ball. His baby jumper from six feet away went up softly and fell through the net cleanly with one second showing on the Kingdome clock.

Michigan 83, Illinois 81. The Wolverines were headed to the national championship game!

Throughout the week leading up to this semifinal meeting, the Wolverines had talked about being a different team from the one that had lost to Illinois earlier. Now, they had proven it. "I felt they played much harder than they usually play," said Anderson. "They played together, a lot more together than I remember during the season. They played a heckuva game."

Bardo said: "They did what they had to do to win the game." Said Vaught: "We felt Illinois was the kind of team that lives and dies on second shots, so we knew we really had to go to the boards and not allow them those second shots." They didn't. The final rebounding tally: Michigan 45, Illinois 39. More to the point: In offensive rebounds, Michigan claimed a 17–13 edge and in second-shot baskets, the Wolverines beat Illinois, 7–5. The Wolverines had, indeed, beaten the Flying Illini at their own game.

Offensively, Rice again was the catalyst, pouring in 28 points. Robinson added 14 while handing off for a mind-boggling 12 assists. Higgins notched 14 points and blocked a pair of shots. Vaught continued to struggle with his shooting, making only 5-of-13 for 10 points. But he was a monster rebounder and a primary reason Michigan was able to negate the Illini's board-crashing tactics: Vaught ripped down an awesome total of 16 rebounds, 12 on the defensive end. Mills added eight points, nine rebounds, and five assists.

In the jubilant Michigan lockerroom, the Wolverines joked about building a new offense based on Mills' missed shots; it was his last two misses which led to Michigan's last five points. "If that's what it takes, I don't care," said an ecstatic Mills.

Virtually lost in the celebration were Mike Griffin and assistant coach Mike Boyd. But Michigan's unsung heroes could take pride, along with Hoop One's Mitch Cauffman, in a job well done. "I think that really helped," Boyd said. "Every move Kendall Gill made, it seemed like Mike Griffin was right there. We felt Mike was in position the whole game through." Added Fisher: "I thought we got terrific play from Mike Griffin today, especially at the defensive end. He did a tremendous job chasing Kendall Gill."

Glen Rice and the Wolverines turned the rebounding table on Illinois the third time around.

Mark Hughes, who finished with nine points and six rebounds, was content to let Higgins bask in the limelight even though his 3-point play down the stretch had been just as critical. "This feels great," grinned the gravel-voiced senior. "One more game to go to complete our mission."

In the post-game press conference, Fisher was asked for perhaps the 1,000th time if it all didn't seem like a dream. "Once again, it sure does," Fisher beamed. "And don't wake me up until Tuesday morning."

Rumeal Decks the Hall

Of course, the inevitable wake-up call came. For Steve Fisher and the Wolverines, it was back to reality quickly. They had two days to prepare for the championship game against Seton Hall, which had handily upset Duke, 95–78, Saturday afternoon. For Michigan players and coaches, the next two days would be a blur of practice, film sessions, and interviews. Mitch Kaufman, who had been up all Saturday night processing tapes of the Illinois game, would continue to get a workout, and so would the Wolverines' patience. "It took a long, long time for that last game to come," Loy Vaught would say later.

On paper—and in the papers—the last game shaped up as a very attractive one. The media had latched onto P.J. Carlesimo's Pirates and Fisher's Wolverines as a pair of Cinderellas headed to the final ball. Michigan was the team with the interim coach, the team trying to overcome the loss of its head coach on the eve of the tournament. The Wolverines, who were seldom highly regarded by the national media under Frieder, had become sentimental favorites under Fisher. He had turned out to be the kind of hero Americans love so much: the humble but talented understudy who, suddenly thrust into the starring role, carries off the part with precision and class. Seton Hall was a team that had never been to the NCAA Tournament before, a team that had been picked to finish near last in the Big East Conference, a team that had been so disappointing the year before that student groups called for Carlesimo to be fired. Largely ignored by media outside the East, the Pirates were now coming across as a gutty bunch of defensive aces. Carlesimo, with his full beard, intelligence, and wit, had emerged as an unusually urbane college coach. Just two months later, he would decline the head coaching job at beleaguered Kentucky.

But while Michigan and Seton Hall were surrounded by compelling circumstances, they hardly qualified as Cinderella teams on the basketball court. Both teams had entered the NCAA Tournament as No. 3 seeds. Michigan had ended the regular season ranked 10th by the Associated Press; Seton Hall was 11th. Both teams had been in the Top 20 virtually all season; Michigan had once been ranked second. Michigan was an outstanding offensive team that was about to lead the nation in field goal percentage for a second straight season, at 56.6 percent, missing an NCAA record by only .75 percent. Seton Hall could also score, averaging 81.8 points. But it was on the defensive end that the Pirates excelled. For the season, they had limited opponents to 68.9 points per game. Advancing along the NCAA tourney trail, they had held Evansville without a field goal in the last seven minutes, they had held Indiana to two in the last eight minutes, and they had limited run-and-gun UNLV to 14 points in the last 13 minutes. In their semifinal win over Duke, the Pirates had spotted the Blue Devils an early 26–8 lead before roaring back to outscore them, 87–52, the rest of the way.

"You've got to respect that," said Terry Mills, and the Wolverines did. They knew that Seton Hall would be a tough matchup. Guards John Morton and Gerald Greene were small at 6–3 and 6–1, respectively, but they were quick, experienced seniors with explosive scoring abilities. Center Ramon Ramos and forward Daryll Walker were a pair of 6–8 wide-bodies who could more than hold their own under the boards. Junior forward Andrew Gaze, a 6–7 Australian, was the Pirates' 3-point threat and a heady player. He and Ramos could pull on the extra experience of having played for their national teams in Australia and Puerto Rico. Seton Hall also had a strong bench, one that had outscored opponents' benches, 98–40, and outrebounded them, 54–30, in five NCAA games. "We've got a team where you can't say stop this guy or that guy and you'll win the game, and so have they," said Fisher. "They're playing a lot like us right now, with tremendous confidence. And they've got outstanding talent."

Carlesimo agreed. "People don't understand how talented our players are," he said. "We have more good players than anyone in the country. That's why we're here. We have to keep Michigan off the boards. We have to get back and make sure they don't score on us in the transition, and we've got to get good pressure and deny the ball from going inside. But I think we're capable of doing that. If we play the way we're capable of playing, the physical matchups are not going to be a problem."

Fisher wasn't so sure. He was especially concerned about Gaze, who could break things open from the outside, and Greene, who would be going up against Rumeal Robinson. Michigan needed another superior defensive job from Griffin, and a long and solid all-around game from Robinson, who knew Greene well from having played against him at Eastern basketball camps.

It was back to the video tube for Griffin, who was given several cutouts of Gaze to study. Over and over, Griffin analyzed the Australian. Where did he like to get the ball? Who screened for him? Did he shoot off the dribble or off the pass? Did he prefer going left or right? Griffin kept studying, perhaps setting himself up for some dreams; on the nights before games, Griffin once explained, he frequently dreamed of basketball. "They're goofy dreams," he said. "Like I'll dream I'm guarding someone and it'll turn out to be George Bush. Just weird stuff. Like I dreamed once that I was coaching the team instead of playing."

In reality, Steve Fisher was doing the coaching. He now had a perfect 5–0 record since taking over for Frieder and, against the backdrop of the Final Four, pressure was mounting for Bo Schembechler to remove the word "interim" from Fisher's title. Pundits everywhere, from lowly newspaper scribes to CBS-TV's Brent Musburger, lampooned Schembechler for dragging his feet. When reporters asked Mills about Fisher's chances to get the job, the big junior deadpanned, "Well, I've never heard of an undefeated coach getting fired, so I'd think his chances are pretty good."

Meanwhile, the man who had been coach watched the whole thing from a distance. Bill Frieder, who had been roundly criticized for the way he left Michigan, journeyed to Seattle for the Final Four, but then he spent most of his time in his hotel room. He was besieged by requests for interviews, most of which he turned down. Knowing that his appearance in the Kingdome would lead to a media circus, he elected to watch the games on his television. As his Wolverines edged Illinois, Frieder acted much as he had at hundreds of Michigan games. With a towel draped over his shoulder, he paced back and forth, jumped out of his seat, yelled at players and officials. Except this time, he was doing it all in his hotel room, alone, yelling at the TV.

"You know that had to be hard for him," Mark Hughes said later. "After all, this was his team. He'd recruited everybody and coached them. To have them get to the Final Four without him. . . . "

"It must have been like seeing your wife going out to dinner with someone else," said Mills.

"It's extremely hard, but what are you going to do?" Frieder said the Sunday morning between games. "I'm not looking back. I did not quit on my team. That was not my decision, it was the football coach's decision. . . . If I could've kept things quiet, I would've. But when it began to leak out I decided to be up front about it. I felt to do otherwise would have been a tremendous distraction for the team." Of the Wolverines' tournament turnabout, Frieder said, "You've got to understand, I think we were headed in that direction as the season progressed. We talked national championship after the Indiana loss. We were playing so well that we almost won in Bloomington, even though we were injured, sick, and battered. We stunk against Illinois, no question about it. But the five games before that were very good. Who knows? Maybe the so-called adversity made them band together. But I'm going to feel we were going to have a good tournament anyway. It's a veteran club, the kind that emerges at tournament time, and everybody is playing well right now."

Frieder said he had talked to several players on the phone during the team's tournament run, and he said he would remain in Seattle for Monday night's championship game, even though he would watch it, too, on TV. It would mark the first time since 1976, when Michigan lost to Indiana in the national final, that Frieder had stayed in a Final Four city for the last game. In all the years since, he had left after the semifinal rounds to get a leg up on recruiting. After Monday's game Janice and Laura Frieder, who had been at every game throughout the tourney, would return to Ann Arbor so Laura could complete school and Janice could sell their home and tie up loose ends. Bill Frieder would head back to Tempe to immerse himself in rebuilding the Sun Devils' program. In the meantime, he had no doubt who would win Monday night's game. "I don't think there's any question they will win it," Frieder said. "And no matter what they say, it's my operation out there."

Steve Fisher and six of the Michigan players killed part of that Sunday by representing the team at a 90-minute press conference. The NCAA required the head coach and all five starters to submit to such interviews. Fisher went them one better by bringing along sixth man Sean Higgins, who had scored the game-winning basket the day before. Higgins would again prove to be a quotable character. Informed that the Wolverines' win had touched off a mini-riot back in Ann Arbor Saturday night, Higgins said, "Well, we'll expect that all the time next year, now that we know they have it in them." Asked how he had slept after the win, Higgins said, "I slept all right, I guess. Except that my face still stings from Coach Fisher slapping on me after the game." Mills had reporters chuckling as he described Fisher's reaction to the win: "He reminded us of that Toyota commercial the way he jumped off the bench." Then there was Mills' description of his last-second miss: "As I was rising up I heard this big yell behind me saying, 'No, no, no! Not that shot!' Maybe that threw me off a little bit."

From the players' standpoint, the highlight of the press conference came from an answer that was never given. A reporter asked both Robinson and Mills to comment on Proposition 48. As Robinson finished his answer, Mills leaned forward, ready to begin his. But before he could, another reporter interrupted with a different question, and Mills was left cut off at the mike. Rice, seated next to Mills, began cracking up. For several minutes he fought to maintain his composure. All the while, Mills was making that hard with a string of deadpan asides. "Oh man, that was so funny," Rice said later. "'T' was all ready to talk. He was leaning into the mike, he was licking his lips, he even had his mouth open. Then they went right past him. I just couldn't handle it."

Meanwhile, Seton Hall players were wondering if they could handle Michigan's size, an attribute that had been somewhat overlooked by the media. As assistant coach Brian Dutcher would note: "It wasn't just our height. Our guys weren't only tall, they were big. We had a lot of beef in there, and I think most teams got pretty worn down trying to bang with us." Seton Hall point guard Gerald Greene certainly was a believer. Asked what impressed him most about Michigan, he said: "Their size. They're huge. They look like football players. They look like they've got some boys from down South who've been eating potatoes all day."

For the rest of Sunday and most of Monday, stuffing themselves with potatoes might have been a welcome diversion for the Wolverines. The closer Monday's 6 P.M. game came, the slower the time seemed to pass. "It seemed like we just sat around all day, wishing we could get out there and play," recalled Loy Vaught. Demetrius Calip started Monday the way he did most days, with a burst of pushups and sprints up and down the hallway outside his hotel room. He spent much of the rest of the day burning off nervous energy by almost constantly dribbling a basketball. Other players flitted from room to room, talking, watching television, lounging around to keep their legs fresh, trying to stay focused on the task at hand without becoming overwhelmed by the enormity of it all.

Rumeal Robinson was especially anxious for the game to begin. Sunday had been a somewhat trying day for him; it had become the day the national media truly discovered Robinson. Over and over, he had been quizzed about Prop 48, about being abandoned as a child, about being adopted by the Fords, about overcoming his learning disability. Over and over, Robinson had to open old wounds and discuss topics that were not only painful, but that he was tired of discussing. The national media were discovering what those who covered the Wolverines regularly had long known: Not only did Robinson have a compelling story to tell, he could tell it well. He was an ingratiating, thoughtful, articulate interview subject. And this weekend, his story had become even more compelling. Helen Ford had journeyed to Seattle along with Robinson's six-year-old brother Louie, whom Robinson called his good luck charm. The Fords couldn't afford to send their whole family, so Louis Ford had remained back in Massachusetts. But on Saturday morning, Ford had been called in on off his mail route to hear some startling news. Well-wishers who knew of the Fords' situation had taken up a collection and had bought him an airplane ticket to Seattle. He had never been on an airplane, he had only seen Robinson play once in college, but he was suddenly on his way to Seattle. However, it was a long trip and Ford was getting a late start. His plane was still in the air as the Michigan-Illinois game began. The pilot put the game on the plane's sound system. A limousine met Ford at the airport. In his first time in a limo, Ford listened to the game as the driver hurried to the Kingdome. Ford finally made it to the arena with a few minutes left in the game. But by the time he found his way inside, by the time he found the rest of his family, the game had ended.

The silver lining was that Louis Ford would have another chance to watch his adopted son perform. Monday night, in the national championship game. If Rumeal Robinson needed any added incentive, he had it.

Steve Fisher began the trip to the most important game of his coaching career by forgetting the pass that identified him as Michigan's head coach. There were a few tense moments when Kingdome security personnel temporarily barred him from the floor. Later Bo Schembechler would joke, "Did he hit somebody? I'd be disappointed if he didn't hit somebody." Fisher didn't, as a NCAA official intervened to smooth the waters.

If the Wolverines were uptight, they weren't showing it. Especially Rice, who needed 25 points to break Bill Bradley's record for a NCAA Tournament and 29 to bypass Mike McGee and become the Big Ten's all-time scoring leader. The unflappable Rice passed the time by climbing onto the trainer's table and taking a half-hour nap.

But there was no sleep in Rice's eyes when he took to the floor before 39,178 fans—the third largest crowd to view a NCAA championship game. Rice hit 5-of-9 first-half shots en route to 13 points as Michigan opened a 37–32 lead at intermission. Robinson was the Wolverines' catalyst with slashing moves to the hoop, playing every minute of the half, scoring 14 points and handing out five assists. Seton Hall guard John Morton had burned the Wolverines for 10 points, but the Pirates had no other player in double figures. Griffin's video sessions were paying off against Gaze. The Australian had scored only two points and had missed all three of his field goal tries—all 3-pointers.

For the first 12 minutes of the second half, the Wolverines did little wrong. Six minutes into the half, Robinson drove the baseline, went under the basket, and came up on the opposite side, seemingly for a reverse layin. Instead, he levitated above the rim and crunched in a reverse, two-handed slam that left fans gasping. Michigan led, 51–39. When Rice cashed in on a 3-point jumper with 8:26 showing, Michigan still owned a 59–49 lead.

Then the Pirates began their comeback. The Wolverines hit a dry spell, one of those stretches that had haunted them earlier in the season, a stretch where they were not only missing their shots, but were settling for quick, perimeter shots rather than working for better ones. Meanwhile, Morton was catching fire. He hit a pair of baskets and converted four free throws in the next two minutes, and with 6:19 left Seton Hall had cut Michigan's lead to 61–59.

Rice pushed Michigan's margin back to five with a 3-pointer. Mills kept it at five by answering two Darryl Walker free throws with an eight-foot banker. But then Greene stole the ball from Robinson and fed Morton for a dunk. Robinson made a bad pass that Gaze picked off, and Morton drilled a baseline jumper. Higgins missed on a 3-point try, Morton snuck inside for a layup, and Seton Hall had the lead, 67–66, with 2:13 remaining.

A Walker free throw put the Pirates up, 68–66, with 1:12 left. Robinson brought the ball down and found Rice on the left wing. With two Pirates leaping at him, Rice rose up and nailed a 3-pointer. Michigan led, 69–68, with 1:06 remaining. A half-minute later, Higgins calmly netted two free throws and Michigan had a 71–68 lead with just 34 seconds left.

But Morton, who would finish with a game-high 35 points, wasn't done yet. With 25 seconds showing, he knocked down a 3-pointer from the left wing to tie the score. After a timeout, the Wolverines got the ball just where they wanted it: in Rice's hands. With one second left, he went up from the top of the key for one more 3-pointer. But his shot hit the rim and fell off.

Overtime! For the first time in 26 years, an extra period would be required to determine the national championship.

In the Michigan huddle, Fisher looked at his troops. They had blown a 12-point lead and a last-second chance to win the game. It would have been natural for them to be dispirited; the momentum that had been theirs for most of the game now seemed to be running Seton Hall's way. So Fisher decided to take another dip into his bag of coaching tricks. Instead of focusing on strategy, he began by telling his players a story. It was a story about a man from California, a man with a reputation for picking winners in athletic events. This man had called Fisher, the coach told his players. He had told him the Wolverines would beat Seton Hall in overtime. And he had said to be certain that Mark Hughes was in the game throughout the overtime.

"I remember thinking 'what in the world is this guy talking about?'" Hughes recalled later. "I was a little shocked. That psychic stuff is a little crazy. But Fish said it honestly and sincerely, and I believed him. He said, 'Okay Mark, I'm going to keep you in. Just go out and play hard. That's all that counts.' Then after the game, he told me it was really a true story."

At the time, some of the Wolverines had their doubts. Noted Mike Griffin: "Fisher had been known to read telegrams from like, unknown people. He will make stuff up. You can tell when he does it because he'll stop in the middle of a telegram that he's supposed to be reading. But this time, as he was telling us, he started shuffling through his notepad like he had written it down. So I sort of started believing it."

Fisher explained his talk succinctly: "I just thought I'd say something stupid to lighten the mood a little bit. It couldn't hurt." Later, the Wolverines would agree that it had helped. "Looking back, it was such a crazy thing to say that it really broke the tension," Loy Vaught said.

Rice made another dent in that tension when he opened the overtime by hitting a jumper from the lane to give Michigan a 73–71 lead. But then Gaze, who had missed all four shots he took during regulation, nailed a 3-pointer to put Seton Hall up, 74–73. Higgins sandwiched a basket and a free throw around a hoop by Walker, and it was a 76–76 game with 2:56 left.

Morton drove another dagger into Michigan's heart by throwing in a 3-pointer just three seconds later, and Seton Hall led, 79–76. With 1:17 remaining, Rice and Higgins missed back-to-back shots. Gerald Greene rebounded and was fouled by Robinson. A 75 percent free throw shooter, Greene had a one-and-one opportunity and the chance to all but clinch the game. But he missed and Mills rebounded. Then Mills came downcourt to hit an 11-foot turnaround that cut Seton Hall's lead to 79–78 with 56 seconds left.

Methodically, the Pirates worked the shot clock down. They got the ball into the hot hands of Morton, who penetrated into the lane for a pull-up jumper. It missed and Rice rebounded with nine seconds showing.

Robinson brought the ball downcourt against Greene, his old summer camp nemesis. Lowering his shoulder, Robinson drove to the right of the paint. Greene was glued to him. Robinson stopped and kicked the ball out to Hughes, who was open and squared away on the right wing. Fisher's prophecy was waiting to come true. But the officials' whistles had sounded. Greene had been called for a blocking foul. With three seconds left, Robinson would go to the line for the one-and-one.

"As soon as he got up to the line, I flashed back to the Wisconsin game," Griffin said later. "Rumeal's been talking about that all year, about how someday he was going to redeem himself."

Robinson had to do some waiting first, as Seton Hall Coach P.J. Carlesimo called a timeout to ice him. In the Wolverines' huddle, J.P. Oosterbaan leaned over Robinson. "No matter what happens, Rumeal," Oosterbaan said, "we'll always love you." As the Wolverines headed back on court, Griffin remembered something Robinson had gotten into the habit of saying in every pre-game huddle. "Just remember Rumeal, God helps those who help themselves," Griffin told him.

In their Kingdome seats, the Ford family looked on anxiously. Earlier in the game they had given out with triumphant cries of "Meal time," their term for when Robinson dominated a game, Now, wearing T-shirts that identified them as "Rumeal's family," they sat breathlessly. It truly was "Meal time."

"I looked at the clock, and there were three seconds left," Robinson recalled. "At first, I thought, 'If I miss this shot, how am I going to get the ball back?' Then it clicked in my mind: 'Forget getting the ball. Just hit the free throws.' It was almost like I came to the end of the game believing that I was supposed to take the last shot. I had no intentions of passing it until they blew the whistle; then, I just sort of passed it on reflex. A coach once told me that, with the game on the line, the easiest thing to do is pass the ball. It seemed I had passed in situations like that earlier in the year. This time I was going to take the last shot.

"The free throws didn't really remind me of the Wisconsin game. Against Seton Hall, I'd already been to the foul line 10 times. I was already warmed up. In the Wisconsin game, I never got to shoot a free throw until the end. This time, I had a lot of concentration. When I got to the foul line the first time, I knew they were going to call a timeout. But it never flashed in my mind that I wasn't going to hit those free throws. I looked at the basket and I thought, 'My dad's come all this way to see this tonight.' Then I was shooting the ball. Coach Fisher said there was a really big flash right in front of me from photographers when I shot. I never even saw it."

What Robinson did see was the basket. And his first shot swishing through it. The game was tied. Seton Hall called another timeout.

"After I made the first one, I knew I was going to make the next one," Robinson said. "I was tired. If I missed, it would be another O.T. I looked over at our bench and I thought, 'We're not going another O.T., I'm too tired.'" Robinson stepped to the line. He eyed the basket. He bounced the ball. He shot.

Another swish. Robinson had not been denied. Michigan led, 80–79.

Two days before, the Wolverines had beaten Illinois to vanquish a couple of ghosts, ghosts of their two previous losses to the Illini and the ghost of their missed shots in the closing seconds of their homecourt loss to Indiana. With his free throws, Robinson had vanquished the ghost of the Wisconsin loss. But Seton Hall had one last chance, and one ghost remained to be exorcised: the ghost of their heartbreaking loss at Bloomington, the ghost of Jay Edwards' buzzer-beating 3-pointer. This time, all the Pirates needed was a two-pointer. They had enough time for one last shot. Seton Hall inbounded the ball and got it downcourt to Walker. With one second left, he rose up on the right side and sent up a 24-footer. It fell short. Rice caught it and then, a second later, caught Robinson in both arms, holding him aloft as they yelled at each other, "We did it! We did it!"

As Bo Schembechler left the Kingdome, he was wearing a big grin. Michigan had just won its first national basketball championship, and in Schembechler's first year as athletic director, the Wolverines had become the first team to win the Rose Bowl and the national basketball crown in the same year. But Schembechler was still playing it coy where Steve Fisher was concerned. "He did a marvelous job. I think we ought to interview Steve Fisher," Schembechler said, "and we will do that."

In the Michigan lockerroom, Fisher continued his low-key approach to the job. "I'll feel disappointed if I don't get it, obviously," he said. "I've been there seven years and I want to stay there another 27. It's a great community and a great university. But that's not my decision."

However, there could be no arguing with the decisions that had been Fisher's to make. Admittedly, his career as a college head coach consisted of only six games. But he was college coaching's only example of perfection, the first rookie coach to ever win the Final Four. "Maybe I should retire unbeaten, untied and unscored upon, and become a ghost writer for you guys," Fisher joked to reporters. With his unlikely surge to the NCAA championship, he certainly had fashioned one of the greatest stories of the 51-year-old tournament. His on-court strategies had been nearly flawless, and his method of calm, positive reinforcement was even more impressive. "I think what impressed me most was Steve's timing," said assistant coach Mike Boyd. "That's a knack that really good coaches have, a knack for calling the right timeouts, for changing things when you should, for knowing when to use different players, how long to rest guys, things like that. I thought Steve had a really exceptional sense of timing throughout the whole tournament. The other thing I thought was really good was the way he made sure that, when we took a kid out, we talked to that kid about what he was doing, what we wanted him to do, and then we told him we'd try to get him back in."

Of course, Fisher had a lot of potent buttons to push. Rice, named the Most Valuable Player of the Final Four, set a new tournament record with 184 points, a 30.6 average. His 75 field goals and 27 3-pointers also set tourney records. By scoring 31 points in the championship victory, Rice ended with 2,442 career points—the most not only in Michigan, but in Big Ten history. Rumeal Robinson was named to the All-Final Four team along with Rice, Seton Hall's Greene and Morton, and Duke's Danny Ferry. Robinson notched a record 11 assists in the title game, and set another Final Four record with a two-game total of 23 assists. Michigan's team total of 42 assists was a Final Four record, and Mills tied a record by blocking three shots in the title game.

Against Seton Hall's relentless defense, Rice had to work extremely hard for his points; he finished with an uncharacteristic 12-of-25 from the field. Still, he capped his career fittingly, leading the Wolverines to the 80–79 win by firing in 31 points and grabbing 11 rebounds. Robinson ended with 21 points, 11 assists, and only five turnovers. Higgins added 10 points, nine rebounds, and a pair of assists. Mills had another strong all-around game with eight points, six rebounds, two assists, three blocked shots, and two steals. Loy Vaught was strong inside, scoring eight points and pulling down seven rebounds. For Seton Hall, Morton poured in 35 points, including four 3-pointers. But the Wolverines held the rest of the Pirates pretty much in check. Greene and Walker finished with 13 apiece, while Ramos got nine. Gaze was taken totally out of his game by Griffin, who later said that playing against European players the previous spring had helped; with Griffin hounding and bumping him relentlessly, Gaze took only five shots, made just one and ended with but five points. In fact, Michigan won the championship game much the same way it won its semifinal over Illinois, by beating the opposition at its own game. Against Seton Hall, that meant defense. The Pirates held Michigan to a meager 44.8 field goal percentage, some 12 percent under the Wolverines' average. But Michigan held Seton Hall to 43.1 percent. Coming into the contest, Michigan was 27–2 when it scored at least 80 points and Seton Hall was 19–0. So the final score of 80–79 was significant. When they had to, the Wolverines had put the lie to another of the knocks that had dogged them: Michigan, never known for its willingness to play defense, had, as Fisher gleefully noted, won the national title with defense.

Meeting with the media offered Steve Fisher a slight diversion from the pressures of coaching in the Final Four.

It would require an overtime period before Brian Dutcher, Steve Fisher, and Mike Boyd had a chance to celebrate their national title.

Walk-on Marc Koenig (30) led the cheers for the Wolverines.

It came down to two free throws—and a chance for redemption—for Rumeal Robinson.

When all was said and done, Steve Fisher could give the thumbs-up to CBS-TV announcer Brent Musburger.

It's definitely a Cinderella celebration in Seattle for the #1 Michigan Wolverines and their fans.

April 3, 1989: Michigan 80, Seton Hall 79
MISSION ACCOMPLISHED!

Michigan's first national basketball championship was greeted by riots in Ann Arbor. The next day, Steve Fisher and the Wolverines were greeted with a riotous welcome home in Crisler Arena.

Michigan Governor James Blanchard was among the thousands who attended the annual Basketball Bust to pay tribute to the Wolverines.

Two Michigan men: the Wolverines' new head coach, Steve Fisher, and Bo Schembechler, athletic director and head football coach.

Rumeal Robinson had to recreate his winning free throws when the Wolverines visited the White House. That's Vice President Dan Quayle helping Steve Fisher show President George Bush how to block out for a rebound.

University of Michigan
1989
N.C.A.A. Champions

By then, there wasn't much force left in the voices of those who had criticized the Wolverines earlier. As Terry Mills said, "I think all those people who criticized us are up in the stands now, with their faces painted maize and blue."

The Michigan lockerroom was a joyous place for a long time that night. "I like this so much," said Sean Higgins, "that I want to come back at least one more time before I graduate." Schembechler, Jack Weidenbach, Michigan president James Duderstadt and scores of family and friends congratulated the victors. Exuberant players granted interview after interview, hugged and joked with each other, and slipped their championship rings on and off with the pride of new brides. But there was one person missing: Bill Frieder. "This game was for Coach Frieder," said Higgins. "Like he said, this is his team. He brought everyone here. This national championship is for him. He should be proud of us." Said Mills: "I think he should be here and be part of all this. He got all these guys and he did a great job. There are no hard feelings. I wish he could come in here now and enjoy this with us." Added Fisher: "It's a difficult, difficult situation for him. I feel badly for the way it happened, but life is funny. Bill told me, 'I couldn't be happier for you.'"

Off in one corner, Rice patiently and repeatedly answered the same questions, continually turning queries about his records and accomplishments into statements of praise for his teammates. Although he had dreamed of playing on a national championship team, Rice said, he had never in his wildest imagination thought of having such an outstanding college career. His only regret, he said somewhat sheepishly, was that he had missed the shot that could've won the game in regulation. "I always dreamed of winning a game with a last-second shot, but I never did it," Rice said. "I couldn't believe I missed that one. I thought sure it was going in."

For Rice, Hughes, and Oosterbaan, the team's only seniors, the title was especially sweet. "Glen and I talked every year since we came here about winning it," said Hughes, "and every year except one, we thought we had the talent to do it. But for some reason, we never got the chemistry right. Until this year. This year the fellows have really been close, on and off the court, and it's been a great thing to be part of."

Gradually, the crowd thinned out. Television cameras, tape recorders, and notebooks began to disappear. Players dressed and filtered out. Fisher, Rice, and Robinson remained the longest, graciously accepting the demands of their newfound superstardom. Finally they, too, left, along with the last manager and the last equipment bag. Behind them, near the center of the lockerroom, stood a chalkboard. On it, someone had written two words:

"Mission accomplished!"

"The Dream Continues"

At Michigan, no matter when the last basketball game is played, the season doesn't really end until the Basketball Bust, the annual awards banquet. In the spring of 1980, the Bust was enlivened by the announcement that Bill Frieder had been hired to succeed Johnny Orr as Michigan's head coach. In the spring of 1989, the scene was strikingly similar. Earlier in the day, Bo Schembechler had called a press conference to announce that he was naming Steve Fisher head coach.

To most observers, Fisher's hiring was a foregone conclusion once he had reached the Final Four. When the Wolverines won the national championship, it seemed there was no way Schembechler could not hire him. But Schembechler wasn't one to rush to judgment. Before he turned the basketball reins over to Fisher on a long-term basis, he wanted to get to know the man a little better. "And I certainly wasn't going to pull him aside to talk for four or five hours while he was in the midst of trying to win the national championship," Schembechler said. So he and Fisher spent three hours together on the Wednesday after the national championship game. Then they spent some more time together on Friday. Schembechler consulted his long-time friend, Bob Knight, who said that he didn't know Fisher well, but that his assistants spoke highly of him. Schembechler satisfied himself that rumors of recruiting violations under Frieder were groundless. Then over the weekend, he made his decision. "I thought Steve Fisher did a helluva job at that tournament, under tough circumstances," Schembechler said. "It was a different Michigan team. They played with enthusiasm. They knew where they were going and they knew what they had to do. I've seen other Michigan teams not respond to tough situations like this group did. Somebody had to be responsible for that and I figure it was Steve Fisher." As for why it took him a week after the championship to name Fisher, Schembechler said, "I was not going to be pressured by the press or by any alumni. I was not going to make an emotional decision. That's not how I work. I wanted it to be cool and calculated. I wanted to study it from every angle. And it always came up Fisher. . . . It's funny, the letters I received Tuesday all said, 'Congratulations, didn't Fisher do a great job?' By Wednesday they were saying, 'What the hell are you waiting for?' By Friday the letters began, 'You SOB, what the hell are you waiting for?' But none of that fazed me."

What did faze Schembechler was more than Fisher's perfect 6–0 record. And it was more than Fisher's image as the ultimate confidence-builder, the image of him as what Seattle columnist Steve Kelley called the Mr. Rogers of college basketball. ("Can you say rebound? I knew you could.") Said Schembechler of Fisher: "I know he comes across as Little Lord Fauntleroy, but I think he can be tough as nails underneath." He also promised to be more of what Schembechler thought a coach should be. Devoted to his wife Angie and sons Mark and Jonathan, Fisher had a much more normal lifestyle than his predecessor. In dress, he tended toward country club casual. Thoughtful and articulate, he wasn't apt to put his foot in his mouth the way Frieder had. "Bill never met the image of a 'Michigan man,'" noted Frieder's old friend, Jerry Ashby. "Steve will fit right in with what Bo wants."

Would Fisher fit in with what Michigan basketball fans wanted? Winning the national title the way he had would undoubtedly earn him a honeymoon and returning six of his top eight players for the next season should help make the honeymoon a long one. But what would happen when the losses came?

"I've been around enough to know that it will never be the same, no matter how much success we have," Fisher said. "It will never again be the same storybook routine we had this season. Even if we should be fortunate enough to win another national championship, it wouldn't be the same. We would be the big bully on the block, not Cinderella like we were this time. I've learned up close and personal that things can turn quickly. I'm no rookie. I've seen it happen to many of my friends. At the Tigers' game the other day I heard the fans boo Willie Hernandez when he came into the game. He struck out two batters and those same fans gave him a standing ovation. I'm well aware of the fickleness of all of us and I believe I'm prepared to handle that."

Said Schembechler: "Steve Fisher is my man and he has my complete support. I believe very strongly that this will begin a new, fresh, exciting era of Michigan basketball." Smiled Fisher: "The dream continues."

In the days and weeks that followed, the Michigan Wolverines discovered what many before them had: that celebrity brings changes, not all of them welcome. The Thursday after the championship, Steve and Angie Fisher dined in the White House as guests of President George Bush. The next week, the whole team jetted to Washington, where it was honored at the U.S. Capitol and at the White House. On a makeshift court arranged in the Rose Garden,

Rumeal Robinson was asked to recreate his title-winning free throws for President Bush. "I hadn't picked up a ball in like, three weeks," Robinson said later. "J.P. (Oosterbaan) bet me $20 I would miss. There were all these people, the President and everyone. I found out that day that I was going to do it, and in a way I was more nervous than against Seton Hall, because I had more time to think about it." But Robinson swished this shot, too. Then he handed the ball to Bush, and the President delighted onlookers by stepping to the line and sinking his own, somewhat more awkward, free throw.

Then it was back to reality. The Wolverines found themselves face-to-face with finals week, made extra-trying by all the class time the team had missed. "Catching up on everything and making it through finals was really, really tough," said Hughes. Making it tougher: the fact that everybody wanted a piece of the Wolverines.

"You want to go a lot of places, but you know you would really be bothered," said Terry Mills. "You try getting away from the basketball scene but everybody wants to talk about it."

Said Loy Vaught: "Sometimes you do get tired of saying the same stuff over and over. When it got to that point, I just stayed home."

Some of the players changed their phone numbers. "You get people who tell you, 'If you need a job or if I can help you in any way, I will,'" noted Mills. "And then you also have people who want you to do things for them," said Hughes. "They might start out saying, 'You probably don't remember me but we were in third grade together, and I just wanted to congratulate you.' Then in a little while they're saying, 'By the way, I wonder if you could. . . .'" Said Mills: "It's like Coach Fisher said, you have to take everything with a grain of salt. We could use people if we wanted to, but we don't want to be a program like that." There was one offer Mills and Hughes regretted declining. "Some guy asked me, Terry, and Rumeal if we wanted to judge a beauty contest," Hughes recalled. "I don't know why, but we turned it down."

Meanwhile, there were the positive aspects of being famous to enjoy.

In June, Rumeal Robinson rode through the streets of Cambridge, Massachusetts, in a parade that was part of "Rumeal Robinson Day." Mark Hughes returned to his alma mater, Muskegon Reeths-Puffer, to speak to community groups on behalf of an effort to build a new high school. Robinson was in demand as a public speaker. But for most of the Wolverines, the increased attention came mostly in the form of everyday contacts which were suddenly made in a whole new way. "Everywhere you go, everybody is proud of you," said Vaught. "And not just around here. I was visiting my girlfriend in Chicago. Even walking around a mall there, people recognized me."

"I don't think my life has changed that much, but you definitely are in the limelight more," said assistant coach Mike Boyd. "You go to the store or anywhere and people are coming up to you, telling you what a great job you did. It used to be that I could walk into a high school and some kids would know me but others would walk right by. Now I go into a high school and a lot of kids, including non-athletes, know me and I'm halfway mobbed."

Walk-on Marc Koenig returned home to Los Angeles and found himself signing autographs. He also was informed that the summer basketball league he played in the year before would guarantee him a spot on a team the next summer, instead of making him try out. Even manager Joel Portnoy found himself a suddenly recognized public figure. Portnoy described the reaction that seemed most common to all those connected with the Wolverines: "Everybody wants to look at the (national championship) ring."

The approach of summer brought the annual scattering of the basketball team. Some of the Wolverines departed Ann Arbor; Mike Griffin was working for a land development firm in New York. But most of the Michigan players remained in Ann Arbor to take classes and work at summer jobs. Demetrius Calip was working for an accounting firm. Loy Vaught had a job as a teacher's aide working with emotionally disturbed youngsters.

Other players, like Glen Rice, virtually disappeared from the local scene. Rice left town much the same way he had eluded defenses all season, vanishing so quickly and quietly that, when the players gathered for a team picture a few days after the championship, they had to leave a chair vacant for their star. Of course, Rice had special reason to be absent. His record-setting tournament performance boosted his professional stock so much that he was taken by the Miami Heat as the fourth pick of the NBA's annual draft. In the weeks leading up to the draft, Rice was criss-crossing the country for personal interviews with NBA teams. But he had another reason to be absent from the Ann Arbor scene: On April 20, Rice had gotten married, surprising many of his teammates by tying the knot with a high school sweetheart, Tracey Cooper, an Army secretary stationed in Maryland.

Meanwhile, Mark Hughes was hoping that Michigan's national championship would enhance his chances of latching onto a NBA career. Those hopes came true when he signed a free-agent contract with the Detroit Pistons.

Fisher, who described the post-championship attention as "mind-boggling," sought relief by taking his family on a long-planned vacation to Disney World. But anonymity proved elusive. The Fishers were made grand marshals of the Magic Kingdom's daily parade, and Fisher posed for pictures with "Cinderella" slipping a basketball shoe on his foot. One of the post-vacation tasks facing him was responding to the thousands of letters which had poured into his office. The letters came from all over, from all sorts of people, including one from a terminally-ill woman who wrote that Michigan's victory had given her courage to fight her own battle.

In the meantime, Fisher was adjusting to his new role. His base salary had risen from $43,000 to $95,000, and with summer camps, a shoe contract, radio and television programs, and speaking engagements, his income was expected to shoot up to approximately $400,000 per year. Fisher had promised to run his own kind of program, but for a while at least, the Wolverines would remain Bill Frieder's team. Frieder had awarded three of the team's four available scholarships to Michigan's three top players the fall before, assuring Fisher of an extremely deep talent pool from which to draw. The next fall would be Fisher's big test as a recruiter, and he would have the prestige of the national championship to aid him.

In Arizona, Frieder faced a different situation. "The players we have coming back wouldn't win a game in the Big Ten," he said ruefully. He was able to bolster those ranks by signing three spring recruits, but one was ineligible under Proposition 48; it would take time to resurrect the Sun Devils. Frieder threw himself into the task with typical abandon, making three or four luncheon appearances a day, talking to every Rotary Club and civic organization that would have him. He abandoned plans to return to Ann Arbor to conduct a summer camp, saying, "I have no desire to compete with Steve. But I would have kept it if they'd hired a Bobby Knight clone." Instead, Frieder remained in Arizona, trying to boost his camp there to 500 participants. In Ann Arbor, Fisher welcomed 1,200 youngsters to his camp.

The early Arizona reviews of Frieder were mixed. "He comes across as kind of a crazy guy," noted one reporter. Many ASU boosters were ecstatic that their school had hired a name coach; many others had been dismayed at how that hiring had been handled. Some observers thought Frieder had his work cut out for him either way. He would have to recruit against popular Arizona coach Lute Olsen. And even when ASU had solid teams in the 1970s, Arizona State fans had been less than supportive, seldom filling more than half their arena's seats. Frieder had a more optimistic view. "The area is phenomenal and the people have been wonderful," he said. "I'm working harder than I ever have in my life, but I'm enjoying it and we're going to get it done here."

Back in Ann Arbor, the Michigan Wolverines were eyeing goals of their own. Rumeal Robinson was working at a rigorous conditioning program including running, swimming, and weightlifting. Mills was making plans to participate in the highly regarded Pete Newell Big Man Camp. Kirk Taylor was plugging away at the difficult task of rehabilitating the injured knee that caused him to undergo surgery in February. Most of the players would spend much of their off-seasons playing in camps and summer leagues, trying to improve their games for the coming season.

They all knew that season could be another great one. Returning would be starters Robinson, Mills, Vaught, and Griffin. Higgins would be expected to step into Rice's spot, and his tournament performance showed that was not an unreasonable expectation. In fact, some observers believed Higgins had the potential to be even better than Rice, because he was bigger and could handle the ball better. Demetrius Calip would be back with some valuable experience under his belt. Taylor wasn't expected back until December, but if he recovered fully he could challenge for a starting spot. Rob Pelinka, who had seen limited action as a freshman, might earn some playing time. Injury-plagued forward Chris Seter was healing, hoping to finally get a chance to show what he could do. Redshirt freshman Eric Riley, a seven-footer who reminded many of a young Roy Tarpley, had the tools to be a pleasant surprise to Michigan fans. Versatile James Voskuil, another redshirt freshman, would vie for playing time. And the three incoming freshmen were promising. Point guard Michael Talley had led Detroit Cooley to three straight state championships, 6–9 forward Sam Mitchell had big man talent, and shooting guard Tony Tolbert was a long-distance sharpshooter who could really fill it up. Expectations would be high again in Ann Arbor, and the schedule would be upgraded accordingly. Gone were the Youngstown States and the South Floridas. In their places, Schembechler's schedule-makers had added Iowa State, Seton Hall, Arizona, Duke, and Marquette. There wouldn't be many cupcakes to fatten up Steve Fisher.

Gradually, things moved closer to normal for Fisher and the Wolverines. The Detroit Pistons drove to the NBA championship, in the process giving the Wolverines a welcome nudge from the limelight. Between visits to NBA teams and prospective agents, Rice dropped in to visit teammates. Graduate assistant Joe Czupek left to join Frieder's staff, but Mike Boyd and Brian Dutcher remained, with Boyd being promoted to chief assistant. Fisher rounded out his staff by hiring Jay Smith, a Kent State assistant who, during his high school days, had scored more points than any other Michigan high school player. "I'll let Jay work with all the guys who can't shoot, but I'm keeping the good ones to myself," Fisher joked.

Fisher knew that the immediate future would be challenging, that every opponent would want to play its best against the defending national champions, that staying on top was usually even harder than getting there in the first place. It had been 17 years since UCLA had been the last team to repeat as college champions, and Fisher wasn't about to pull a Pat Riley and guarantee a repeat. "The key will be how hard the kids work in the off-season," Fisher said. "But we have good kids and I think they'll wear that crown proudly and try to defend it."

As spring turned into summer, the Wolverines found that they were pinching themselves less and less often. "But every once in a while, I just sit at home and think about it," said Mills. "And I say to myself, 'You know, we did it. We actually won the national title.'"

One afternoon, Rumeal Robinson and Loy Vaught got together for lunch. They talked of what it had been like to win the national championship, and their talk naturally drifted toward the coming season. "All of a sudden we looked at each other, and we knew we were both thinking the same thing," Vaught said. "We looked at each other and we said, 'You know what? We could just do it again.'"

The dream continued.

Season Statistics

HONORS

Glen Rice
NCAA Tournament MVP
NCAA All-Tournament Team
Southeast Regional MVP
All-Southeast Regional Team
Chicago Tribune Silver Basketball
UPI Big Ten MVP
AP-UPI All-Big Ten
Bill Buntin Award
(Team Most Valuable Player)
Team Co-Captain

Sean Higgins
All-Southeast Regional Team

Rumeal Robinson
NCAA All-Tournament Team
All-Southeast Regional Team
AP Third Team All-Big Ten
UPI Hon. Mention All-Big Ten
Wayman Britt Award
(Best "M" Defensive Player)

Loy Vaught
AP Third Team All-Big Ten
UPI Hon. Mention All-Big Ten
"M" Outstanding Rebounder Award

Mark Hughes
Thad Garner Leadership Award
Team Co-Captain

Terry Mills
Rudy Tomjanovich Award
("M" Most Improved Player)

Mike Griffin
Steve Grote Hustler Award

Demetrius Calip
Rudy Tomjanovich Award
("M" Most Improved Player)

1988-89 RESULTS

U-M	FG%	OPPONENT	OPP	FG%	HIGH SCORE	HIGH REB	ATT	DATE	PLACE
91	63.2	Vanderbilt	66	41.9	18 Rice	6 Rice, Griffin	3,000	11/25	Maui Classic
79	61.5	Memphis State	75	50.9	29 Rice	6 Vaught	3,000	11/26	Maui Classic
91	62.5	Oklahoma	80	47.7	20 Robinson	9 Vaught	3,000	11/27	Maui Classic
102	57.6	GRAMBLING ST.	62	35.1	23 Rice	9 Mills, Vaught	12,409	12/2	Ann Arbor
104	61.5	SOUTH DAKOTA ST.	66	37.0	24 Vaught	11 Vaught	12,511	12/3	Ann Arbor
98	57.4	TAMPA	65	42.3	29 Rice	9 Rice	11,197	12/5	Ann Arbor
108	60.6	CENTRAL MICHIGAN	62	29.2	21 Rice	10 Rice	12,434	12/7	Ann Arbor
107	61.8	Western Michigan	60	33.9	28 Rice 1	2 Hughes	8,250	12/10	Kalamazoo, MI
80	50.0	EASTERN MICHIGAN	57	38.2	18 Higgins	8 Vaught	12,208	12/12	Ann Arbor
125	61.5	NORTHERN MICHIGAN	75	44.9	36 Rice	13 Mills	11,203	12/20	Ann Arbor
121	67.6	YOUNGSTOWN STATE	72	41.7	30 Rice	10 Vaught	12,175	12/21	Ann Arbor
66	47.5	Alaska-Anchorage	70	62.8	24 Rice	9 Rice, Mills	11,400	12/28	Salt Lake City
100	51.4	Holy Cross	63	41.3	28 Rice	11 Mills	11,514	12/29	Salt Lake City
94	59.0	NORTHWESTERN	66	51.0	25 Rice	11 Vaught	13,570	1/7	Ann Arbor
98	63.6	MINNESOTA	83	43.8	31 Rice	7 Rice	13,055	1/12	Ann Arbor
84	51.5	Illinois	96	50.0	30 Rice	9 Rice	16,499	1/14	Champaign, IL
99	64.1	OHIO STATE	73	42.3	23 Rice, Mills	10 Hughes	13,191	1/16	Ann Arbor
68	52.2	Wisconsin	71	49.0	25 Rice	9 Mills	11,174	1/21	Madison, WI
70	49.1	INDIANA	71	55.1	19 Rice	14 Vaught	13,609	1/23	Ann Arbor
99	66.7	Purdue	88	58.3	34 Rice	7 Rice	14,123	1/29	W. Lafayette, IN
82	58.7	MICHIGAN STATE	66	46.8	29 Rice	10 Rice	13,609	2/4	Ann Arbor
108	41.8	OT Iowa	107	51.2	24 Rice	14 Vaught	15,500	2/9	Iowa City, IA
80	58.8	Minnesota	88	53.2	29 Rice	7 Vaught	15,439	2/11	Minneapolis, MN
84	59.3	PURDUE	70	45.0	21 Rice	8 Vaught	13,609	2/16	Ann Arbor
75	53.4	Indiana	76	52.7	24 Robinson	10 Vaught	17,311	2/19	Bloomington, IN
89	54.8	Ohio State	72	35.2	30 Rice	12 Vaught	13,276	2/23	Columbus, OH
92	63.5	WISCONSIN	70	43.3	38 Rice	11 Vaught	13,504	2/25	Ann Arbor
79	63.5	Michigan State	52	38.6	16 Vaught	8 Mills	10,004	2/27	East Lansing
119	62.9	IOWA	96	50.0	33 Rice	7 Rice, Mills	13,519	3/4	Ann Arbor
88	56.7	Northwestern	79	50.0	26 Rice	9 Rice	7,624	3/9	Evanston, IL
73	42.3	ILLINOIS	89	60.7	22 Robinson	12 Vaught	13,609	3/11	Ann Arbor
92	55.2	Xavier	87	52.3	23 Robinson, Rice	10 Hughes	12,349	3/17	Atlanta
91	59.7	South Alabama	82	42.9	36 Rice	8 Rice	12,821	3/19	Atlanta
92	54.5	North Carolina	87	53.0	34 Rice	6 4 players	22,314	3/23	Lexington, KY
102	58.6	Virginia	65	38.1	32 Rice	9 Vaught	22,755	3/25	Lexington, KY
83	46.8	Illinois	81	44.8	28 Rice	16 Vaught	39,187	4/1	Seattle, WA
80	44.8	OT Seton Hall	79	43.1	31 Rice	11 Rice	39,187	4/3	Seattle, WA

TEAM RECORD: ALL GAMES 30-7 (81.0%); LEAGUE 12-6 (66.6%); TOURNAMENT 6-0 (100.0%)

MISSION ACCOMPLISHED!

INDIVIDUAL STATISTICS

NAME	G	ST	TOTAL FG			3-PT FG			FREE THROWS			REBOUNDS				PF	DIS	AST	TO	BLK	STL	AVG MIN	PTS	AVG
			FG	FGA	PCT	FG	FGA	PCT	FT	FTA	PCT	OFF	DEF	TOT	AVG									
Rice	37	37	363	629	57.7	99	192	51.6	124	149	83.2	77	155	232	6.3	75	1	85	81	11	39	34	949	25.6
Robinson	37	36	199	357	55.7	30	64	46.9	122	186	65.6	31	94	125	3.4	105	5	233	131	4	70	30	550	14.9
Vaught	37	21	201	304	66.1	2	5	40.0	63	81	77.8	94	202	296	8.0	94	3	36	50	11	19	23	467	12.6
Mills	37	37	180	319	56.4	0	2	.0	70	91	76.9	74	144	218	5.9	95	3	104	77	49	20	27	430	11.6
Higgins	34	16	158	312	50.6	51	110	46.4	54	70	77.1	31	76	107	3.1	76	2	51	60	11	10	23	421	12.4
Hughes	35	4	104	171	60.8	1	2	50.0	29	48	60.4	41	101	142	4.1	58	0	40	26	7	12	20	238	6.8
Griffin	37	31	33	65	50.8	0	2	.0	33	43	76.7	24	65	89	2.4	104	3	103	56	9	24	23	99	2.7
Taylor	21	2	33	69	47.8	7	18	38.9	22	36	61.1	12	34	46	2.2	30	1	46	23	6	20	17	95	4.5
Calip	30	0	22	50	44.0	2	9	22.2	14	17	82.4	5	14	19	.6	19	0	25	23	0	7	7	60	2.0
Oosterbaan	22	0	22	39	56.4	0	1	.0	9	13	69.2	9	17	26	1.2	15	0	11	9	3	0	5	53	2.4
Pelinka	26	1	9	25	36.0	4	14	28.6	7	10	70.0	5	10	15	.6	7	0	10	12	2	3	4	29	1.1
Koenig	7	0	1	1	100.0	0	0	.0	0	0	.0	0	1	1	.1	1	0	1	3	0	2	1	2	.3
TOTAL	37	37	1325	2341	56.6	196	419	46.8	547	744	73.5	403	992	1395	37.7	679	18	745	557	113	226		3393	91.7
OPP	37	37	1055	2322	45.4	164	466	35.2	493	710	69.4	395	726	1121	30.3	705	15	514	578	36	237		2767	74.8

*Statistics include all 37 games

NCAA TOURNAMENT GAME BOXSCORES

March 17, 1989
THE OMNI
Atlanta, Georgia

Michigan (92)

No.	Player	Total FG FG	Total FG FGA	3-Pts FG	3-Pts FGA	FT	FTA	Reb O	Reb - D	PF	Pts	A	TO	Bk	S	Min
41	Rice, Glen	9	22	5	9	0	0	1	2	2	23	2	3	1	0	40
52	Mills, Terry	8	12	0	0	2	2	2	4	4	18	5	1	1	2	32
35	Vaught, Loy	2	4	0	0	0	0	1	2	4	4	0	0	0	0	10
20	Griffin, Mike	0	0	0	0	0	0	0	0	2	0	2	0	0	1	19
21	Robinson, Rumeal	8	13	1	2	6	9	2	2	4	23	8	6	1	2	34
55	Hughes, Mark	4	5	0	0	0	1	5	5	2	8	0	0	0	2	28
24	Higgins, Sean	3	6	0	1	1	1	0	3	2	7	0	4	0	1	23
13	Calip, Demetrius	3	5	0	0	3	3	2	0	1	9	1	3	0	0	14
	TOTALS	37	67	6	12	12	16	14	19	21	92	18	17	3	8	200

Team rebounds included in totals

Total field-goal percentages: 1st half 17/29 58.6% 2nd half 20/38 52.6% Game 37/67 55.2%
3-point percentages: 1st half 4/8 50.0% 2nd half 2/4 50.0% Game 6/12 50.0%
Free-Throw percentages: 1st half 4/4 100.0% 2nd half 8/12 66.7% Game 12/16 75.0%

Xavier (87)

No.	Player	Total FG FG	Total FG FGA	3-Pts FG	3-Pts FGA	FT	FTA	Reb O	Reb - D	PF	Pts	A	TO	Bk	S	Min
30	Parker, Colin	0	1	0	0	0	0	0	0	0	0	2	0	0	0	
42	Hill, Tyrone	7	12	0	0	7	7	3	3	4	21	2	3	0	0	
33	Strong, Derek	8	12	0	0	2	3	4	6	3	18	0	8	0	1	
11	Kimbrough, Stan	5	16	2	4	1	2	2	3	4	13	6	1	0	2	
20	Davenport, M.	6	13	0	4	3	4	1	1	3	15	1	2	0	2	
10	Walker, Jamal	6	9	1	1	3	5	2	0	3	16	9	4	0	2	
31	Minor, Dave	2	2	0	0	0	0	0	1	1	4	1	1	0	0	
15	Raeford, Sydney	0	0	0	0	0	0	0	0	1	0	0	0	0	0	
	TOTALS	34	65	3	9	16	21	12	18	19	87	21	19	0	7	

Team rebounds included in totals

Total field-goal percentages: 1st half 19/34 55.9% 2nd half 15/31 48.4% Game 34/65 52.3%
3-point percentages: 1st half 3/6 50.0% 2nd half 0/3 0.0% Game 3/9 33.3%
Free-Throw percentages: 1st half 4/5 80.0% 2nd half 12/16 75.0% Game 16/21 76.2%

Score by halves: Michigan 42 - 50 = 92 Xavier 45 - 42 = 87 Technicals: None Attendance: 12,349

March 19, 1989
THE OMNI
Atlanta, Georgia

Michigan (91)

No.	Player	Total FG FG	FGA	3-Pts FG	FGA	FT	FTA	Reb O	- D	PF	Pts	A	TO	Bk	S	Min
41	Rice, Glen	16	25	3	7	1	1	2	6	2	36	5	4	0	1	37
55	Hughes, Mark	2	4	0	0	0	0	2	2	3	4	0	0	1	1	24
52	Mills, Terry	9	13	0	0	6	8	2	5	3	24	5	3	0	0	38
20	Griffin, Mike	2	2	0	0	0	0	0	1	3	4	0	2	0	0	24
21	Robinson, Rumeal	5	8	1	2	1	2	0	1	4	12	5	3	0	3	27
35	Vaught, Loy	1	5	0	0	0	0	1	6	3	2	0	0	0	0	13
13	Calip, Demetrius	0	1	0	0	3	4	0	1	2	3	5	1	0	0	19
24	Higgins, Sean	2	4	0	1	2	2	0	2	2	6	2	1	0	0	17
25	Pelinka, Rob	0	0	0	0	0	0	0	0	0	0	0	1	0	0	1
	TOTALS	37	62	4	10	13	17	7	25	22	91	22	15	1	5	200

Team rebounds included in totals

Total field-goal percentages:	1st half	20/33	60.6%	2nd half	17/29	58.6%	Game 37/62 59.7%
3-point percentages:	1st half	2/4	50.0%	2nd half	2/6	33.3%	Game 4/10 40.0%
Free-Throw percentages:	1st half	2/3	66.7%	2nd half	11/14	78.6%	Game 13/17 76.5%

South Alabama (82)

No.	Player	Total FG FG	FGA	3-Pts FG	FGA	FT	FTA	Reb O	- D	PF	Pts	A	TO	Bk	S	Min
13	Estaba, Gabriel	7	15	0	1	1	3	4	5	4	15	2	3	0	1	37
24	Jimmerson, John	3	5	0	0	1	2	2	2	1	7	5	4	0	0	22
42	Darden, Phillip	0	0	0	0	0	0	0	3	4	0	0	0	1	0	9
05	Hodge, Jeff	6	14	3	9	1	1	1	2	1	16	2	1	0	0	37
11	Lewis, Junie	9	17	0	2	7	10	6	3	1	25	3	4	0	0	37
21	Smith, Neil	4	8	0	0	6	7	5	2	4	14	0	1	0	0	27
32	Brodnick, T.	1	7	1	4	2	2	0	2	1	5	6	2	0	0	23
12	Turner, Derek	0	4	0	3	0	0	0	1	1	0	0	0	0	0	7
25	Nelson, Darrell	0	0	0	0	0	0	0	0	0	0	0	0	0	1	1
	TOTALS	30	70	4	19	18	25	19	20	17	82	18	15	1	2	200

Team rebounds included in totals

Total field-goal percentages:	1st half	15/34	44.1%	2nd half	15/36	41.7%	Game 30/70 42.9%
3-point percentages:	1st half	2/12	16.7%	2nd half	2/7	28.6%	Game 4/19 21.1%
Free-Throw percentages:	1st half	15/21	71.4%	2nd half	3/4	75.0%	Game 18/25 72.0%

Score by halves: Michigan 44 - 47 = 91 South Alabama 47 - 35 = 82 Technicals: None Attendance: 12,821

March 23, 1989
RUPP ARENA
Lexington, Kentucky

Michigan (92)

No.	Player	Total FG FG	Total FG FGA	3-Pts FG	3-Pts FGA	FT	FTA	Reb O	Reb - D	PF	Pts	A	TO	Bk	S	Min
41	Rice, Glen	13	19	8	12	0	0	1	5	1	34	2	2	0	1	37
52	Mills, Terry	8	11	0	0	0	2	1	5	3	16	1	3	1	1	33
35	Vaught, Loy	1	3	0	0	2	2	0	6	5	4	0	3	2	1	23
20	Griffin, Mike	0	1	0	0	0	0	1	0	1	0	1	1	0	0	8
21	Robinson, Rumeal	7	15	3	6	0	2	3	2	3	17	13	5	0	1	37
24	Higgins, Sean	5	11	2	5	2	2	0	2	0	14	3	1	0	1	21
13	Calip, Demetrius	1	4	0	1	0	0	0	1	1	2	0	1	0	1	21
55	Hughes, Mark	1	2	0	0	3	4	3	3	4	5	0	3	1	0	20
	TOTALS	36	66	13	24	7	12	9	25	18	92	20	19	4	6	200

Team rebounds included in totals

Total field-goal percentages: 1st half 20/34 58.8% 2nd half 16/32 50.0% Game 36/66 54.5%
3-point percentages: 1st half 6/11   54.5% 2nd half 7/13   53.8% Game 13/24 54.2%
Free-Throw percentages: 1st half 4/5   80.0% 2nd half 3/7   42.9% Game 7/12   58.3%

North Carolina (87)

No.	Player	Total FG FG	Total FG FGA	3-Pts FG	3-Pts FGA	FT	FTA	Reb O	Reb - D	PF	Pts	A	TO	Bk	S	Min
20	Bucknall, Steve	2	7	2	4	4	4	2	5	1	10	10	4	0	3	36
22	Madden, Kevin	5	12	0	2	0	0	1	0	1	10	0	0	1	2	25
42	Williams, Scott	4	9	0	0	0	0	1	4	1	8	0	2	0	2	28
14	Lebo, Jeff	6	10	5	9	2	2	1	0	3	19	7	2	0	0	32
21	Rice, King	1	3	0	1	2	2	0	1	0	4	4	2	0	2	14
34	Reid, J.R.	12	18	0	0	2	7	1	5	4	26	0	2	0	0	29
44	Fox, Rick	4	5	0	0	0	0	0	2	2	8	3	2	0	2	27
32	Chilcutt, Pete	1	2	0	0	0	0	0	4	2	2	0	0	0	0	9
	TOTALS	35	66	7	16	10	15	7	24	14	87	24	14	1	11	200

Team rebounds included in totals

Total field-goal percentages: 1st half 20/33 60.6% 2nd half 15/33 45.5% Game 35/66 53.0%
3-point percentages: 1st half 7/10   70.0% 2nd half 0/6   0.0%   Game 7/16   43.8%
Free-Throw percentages: 1st half 0/2   0.0%   2nd half 10/13 76.9% Game 10/15 66.7%

Score by halves: Michigan 50 - 42 = 92 North Carolina 47 - 40 = 87 Technicals: None Attendance: 22,314

March 25, 1989
RUPP ARENA
Lexington, Kentucky

Michigan (102)

No.	Player	Total FG		3-Pts		FT	FTA	Reb		PF	Pts	A	TO	Bk	S	Min
		FG	FGA	FG	FGA			O	D							
41	Rice, Glen	13	16	4	5	2	2	0	6	3	32	2	3	0	2	32
52	Mills, Terry	4	9	0	0	0	0	0	5	2	8	2	1	0	1	27
35	Vaught, Loy	4	6	0	0	0	1	2	7	3	8	2	0	0	0	21
20	Griffin, Mike	0	1	0	0	0	0	0	0	4	0	3	0	0	1	22
21	Robinson, Rumeal	5	9	0	1	3	3	1	2	2	13	7	2	0	1	23
13	Calip, Demetrius	2	3	0	0	2	2	0	5	2	6	5	2	0	0	22
24	Higgins, Sean	11	15	7	10	2	3	1	2	2	31	0	0	0	0	20
55	Hughes, Mark	1	4	0	0	0	0	0	7	4	2	2	1	0	0	20
54	Oosterbaan, J.P.	1	3	0	1	0	1	0	3	1	2	0	0	0	0	6
25	Pelinka, Rob	0	4	0	3	0	0	0	0	0	0	0	1	0	0	5
30	Koenig, Marc	0	0	0	0	0	0	0	0	0	0	0	1	0	2	2
	TOTALS	41	70	11	20	9	12	6	37	23	102	23	11	0	7	200

Team rebounds included in totals

Total field-goal percentages: 1st half 19/33 57.6% 2nd half 22/37 59.5% Game 41/70 58.6%
3-point percentages: 1st half 4/7 57.1% 2nd half 7/13 53.8% Game 11/20 55.0%
Free-Throw percentages: 1st half 2/3 66.7% 2nd half 7/9 77.8% Game 9/12 75.0%

Virginia (65)

No.	Player	Total FG		3-Pts		FT	FTA	Reb		PF	Pts	A	TO	Bk	S	Min
		FG	FGA	FG	FGA			O	D							
20	Stith, Bryant	3	6	1	1	2	4	0	3	3	9	1	2	0	1	33
30	Blundin, Matt	1	1	0	0	0	0	2	2	1	2	2	3	0	0	21
32	Dabbs, Brent	5	10	0	0	2	4	3	9	2	12	0	1	0	1	37
11	Morgan, Richard	5	18	3	9	2	2	0	1	1	15	0	3	0	1	26
22	Crotty, John	5	13	2	3	2	4	0	3	1	14	7	2	0	0	36
24	Katstra, Dirk	3	9	1	6	0	0	0	2	2	7	1	2	1	2	13
44	Daniel, Jeff	0	1	0	0	0	2	0	3	4	0	1	0	0	0	13
12	Turner, Kenny	1	1	0	0	0	1	1	0	0	2	0	0	0	0	6
21	Williams, C.	0	1	0	0	0	3	0	0	0	0	0	0	0	0	8
10	Oliver, Anthony	0	0	0	0	1	2	1	1	2	1	0	2	0	0	4
31	Cooke, Mark	1	3	1	3	0	0	1	0	0	3	0	0	0	0	3
	TOTALS	24	63	8	22	9	22	9	24	16	65	12	15	1	5	200

Team rebounds included in totals

Total field-goal percentages: 1st half 10/28 35.7% 2nd half 14/35 40.0% Game 24/63 38.1%
3-point percentages: 1st half 2/10 20.0% 2nd half 6/12 50.0% Game 8/22 36.4%
Free-Throw percentages: 1st half 3/6 50.0% 2nd half 6/16 37.5% Game 9/22 40.9%

Score by halves: Michigan 44 - 58 = 102 Virginia 25 - 40 = 65 Technicals: None Attendance: 22,755

April 1, 1989
THE KINGDOME
Seattle, Washington

Michigan (83)

No.	Player	Total FG FG	Total FG FGA	3-Pts FG	3-Pts FGA	FT	FTA	Reb O	Reb - D	PF	Pts	A	TO	Bk	S	Min
41	Rice, Glen	12	24	2	4	2	2	3	2	1	28	1	0	0	3	37
52	Mills, Terry	4	8	0	0	0	0	3	6	4	8	5	2	1	0	31
35	Vaught, Loy	5	13	0	0	0	0	4	12	2	10	0	0	0	0	29
20	Griffin, Mike	0	1	0	0	0	0	0	1	2	0	3	1	0	2	17
21	Robinson, Rumeal	6	13	0	1	2	5	1	0	4	14	12	5	0	1	40
55	Hughes, Mark	4	5	0	0	1	1	1	5	3	9	1	2	0	0	19
24	Higgins, Sean	5	12	1	3	3	3	2	1	2	14	1	2	2	0	24
13	Calip, Demetrius	0	1	0	0	0	0	0	0	2	0	0	0	0	0	3
	TOTALS	36	77	3	8	8	11	17	28	20	83	23	12	3	6	200

Team rebounds included in totals

Total field-goal percentages:	1st half	17/39	43.6%	2nd half	19/38	50.0%	Game 36/77 46.8%
3-point percentages:	1st half	2/5	40.0%	2nd half	1/3	33.3%	Game 3/8 37.5%
Free-Throw percentages:	1st half	3/4	75.0%	2nd half	5/7	71.4%	Game 8/11 72.7%

Illinois (81)

No.	Player	Total FG FG	Total FG FGA	3-Pts FG	3-Pts FGA	FT	FTA	Reb O	Reb - D	PF	Pts	A	TO	Bk	S	Min
25	Anderson, Nick	6	14	0	1	5	6	3	4	1	17	2	2	0	2	35
33	Battle, Kenny	10	17	1	1	8	10	4	3	2	29	1	1	1	0	40
45	Hamilton, Lowell	5	14	0	0	1	2	1	8	5	11	0	1	0	1	34
13	Gill, Kendall	5	9	0	2	1	1	1	3	1	11	2	1	0	3	40
35	Bardo, Steve	1	7	1	3	4	4	2	4	3	7	8	5	1	0	32
23	Smith, Larry	3	5	0	1	0	0	0	2	2	6	1	1	0	0	18
24	Small, Ervin	0	0	0	0	0	0	0	0	2	0	0	0	0	0	6
30	Liberty, Marcus	0	1	0	0	0	0	0	0	0	0	0	0	0	0	5
	TOTALS	30	67	2	8	19	23	13	26	16	81	14	11	2	6	200

Team rebounds included in totals

Total field-goal percentages:	1st half	12/32	37.5%	2nd half	18/35	51.4%	Game 30/67 44.8%
3-point percentages:	1st half	1/5	20.0%	2nd half	1/3	33.3%	Game 2/8 25.0%
Free-Throw percentages:	1st half	13/16	81.3%	2nd half	6/7	85.7%	Game 19/23 82.6%

Score by halves: Michigan 39 - 44 = 83 Illinois 38 - 43 = 81 Technicals: None Attendance: 39,187

MISSION ACCOMPLISHED!

April 3, 1989
THE KINGDOME
Seattle, Washington

Michigan (80)

No.	Player	Total FG FG	Total FG FGA	3-Pts FG	3-Pts FGA	FT	FTA	Reb O	Reb - D	PF	Pts	A	TO	Bk	S	Min
41	Rice, Glen	12	25	5	12	2	2	1	10	2	31	0	2	0	0	42
52	Mills, Terry	4	8	0	0	0	0	3	3	2	8	2	2	3	2	34
35	Vaught, Loy	4	8	0	0	0	0	2	5	2	8	0	2	0	1	26
20	Griffin, Mike	0	0	0	0	0	0	2	2	4	0	3	2	0	0	17
21	Robinson, Rumeal	6	13	0	0	9	10	1	2	2	21	11	5	0	0	43
24	Higgins, Sean	3	10	1	4	3	4	2	7	3	10	2	1	1	0	27
55	Hughes, Mark	1	1	0	0	0	0	0	2	2	2	0	0	0	0	25
13	Calip, Demetrius	0	2	0	0	0	0	0	0	3	0	1	0	0	0	11
	TOTALS	30	67	6	16	14	16	12	33	20	80	19	14	4	3	225

Team rebounds included in totals

Total field-goal percentages:	1st half	15/30	50.0%	2nd half	15/37	40.5%	Game	30/67	44.8%
3-point percentages:	1st half	1/3	33.3%	2nd half	5/13	38.5%	Game	6/16	37.5%
Free-Throw percentages:	1st half	6/6	100.0%	2nd half	8/10	80.0%	Game	14/16	87.5%

Seton Hall (79)

No.	Player	Total FG FG	Total FG FGA	3-Pts FG	3-Pts FGA	FT	FTA	Reb O	Reb - D	PF	Pts	A	TO	Bk	S	Min
10	Gaze, Andrew	1	5	1	5	2	2	2	1	3	5	3	2	0	1	39
24	Walker, Darryll	5	9	0	1	3	4	3	8	2	13	1	2	0	0	39
25	Ramos, Ramon	4	9	0	0	1	1	0	5	2	9	1	1	1	1	33
15	Greene, Gerald	5	13	2	5	1	3	0	5	3	13	5	2	0	2	43
23	Morton, John	11	26	4	12	9	10	1	3	3	35	3	3	0	0	37
31	Cooper, Michael	0	0	0	0	0	0	0	2	1	0	0	1	1	0	14
32	Avent, Anthony	1	2	0	0	0	0	1	2	0	2	1	0	0	0	11
30	Volcy, Frantz	0	0	0	0	0	2	0	1	2	0	0	0	0	0	7
04	Wigington, Pookey	1	1	0	0	0	0	0	0	1	2	0	0	0	0	2
	TOTALS	28	65	7	23	16	22	9	27	17	79	14	11	2	4	225

Team rebounds included in totals

Total field-goal percentages:	1st half	13/32	40.6%	2nd half	15/33	45.5%	Game	28/65	43.1%
3-point percentages:	1st half	4/14	28.6%	2nd half	3/9	33.3%	Game	7/23	30.4%
Free-Throw percentages:	1st half	2/4	50.0%	2nd half	14/18	77.8%	Game	16/22	72.7%

Score by halves: Michigan 37 - 34 - 9 (OT) = 80   Seton Hall 32 - 39 - 8 (OT) = 79
Technicals: None   Attendance: 39,187